FROM MARRIAGE TO DIVORCE

Georges Feydeau

FROM MARRIAGE TO DIVORCE

BETTER LATE
ONE MONTH EARLY
TAKE YOUR MEDICINE LIKE A MAN
DON'T WALK ABOUT WITH NOTHING ON

Translated by Peter Meyer

OBERON BOOKS
LONDON

First published in 1998 by Oberon Books Ltd (incorporating Absolute Classics), 521 Caledonian Road, London, N7 9RH. Tel 0171 607 3637 / Fax: 0171 607 3629

British Library Cataloguing-in-Publication Data
A catalogue record for this book is available from the British Library.

ISBN 1 870259 70 X

Cover design: Andrzej Klimowski

Cover Typography: Richard Doust

Printed in Great Britain by Arrowhead Books, Reading

Contents

INTRODUCTION

When Feydeau left school in 1879, he began to write monologues for performance by leading actors and actresses in salons and at charity concerts, but by 1882 he had progressed to the one-act play, which he continued to write throughout his career. The most successful were the four translated in this volume, written between 1908 and 1911 and which he always wished to see published together under the title *From Marriage To Divorce.* They were more or less based on the breakdown of his own marriage and indeed his son Jacques said the episode in *On Purge Bébé* was almost a direct account of an actual event.

In 1889 Feydeau had married Marianne Carolus Duran, the daughter of a fashionable portrait painter and three years later he had his first great success in the theatre. He then began to make a great deal of money, but incurred heavy losses, gambling on the stock exchange, and was forced to sell part of his wife's dowry. She was a beautiful woman who bore him four children, but, at any rate in later years, he would spend the evening with friends, leaving her at home alone, so it is not surprising she was grossly extravagant. Although she had a difficult life, she too cannot have been an easy person to live with, to judge from the portrait he drew of her in these four plays.

In 1909, after a particularly violent quarrel, he left home and in 1914 Marianne sued for divorce, obtaining it eighteen months later.

In 1941 *Feu La Mère De Madame* was the first of Feydeau's plays to be staged by the Comedie Française. Madeleine Renaud played the lead and it was no doubt her success in this which induced the Renaud-Barrault company to produce *Occupe Toi D'Amélie* in 1948. A critic then noted that Barrault, in using a classical company, had imposed upon the play a new style, which justified including it in repertory with Marivaux and Shakespeare. This is the style to which we have become further accustomed by the productions of the Comedie Francaise and the National Theatre and which have resulted in Feydeau being accepted as the greatest French comic dramatist since Molière.

These translations were commissioned by BBC Radio and first broadcast in 1973. The director was Glyn Dearman and the chief characters were played by Jill Bennett and John Osborne. This was the first time he had acted on radio, and it should be recorded that there could not have been a nicer actor to work with.

Peter Meyer
London, 1998

BETTER LATE

Feu la mère de madame

Characters

YVONNE

LUCIEN, her husband

ANNETTE, their maid

JOSEPH, a manservant

*Y*VONNE's bedroom in Paris about 1910. A modest room with an attempt at elegance and comfort: cheap luxury, pleasant but valueless ornaments. On the wall, framed modern engravings, Japanese fans etc. In the back wall, a door into the hall. Midstage right, a doorway, with the door removed and replaced by a curtain. Midstage left, in a wall at an angle, the door of LUCIEN's room. Downstage left, a fireplace with a mirror above it. Downstage right, a bed, extending towards the centre of the stage, with a stool, as long as the width of the bed, against its foot. At the head of the bed, downstage, a small table with a nightlight, which is burning, and a medicine bottle. At the head of the bed, on the other side, an armchair. Against the wall, between the hall door and the door to LUCIEN's room, a small lady's bureau, open. On its right, a chair against the wall. Near the fireplace, almost in front of the proscenium, an armchair with its back slightly towards the audience: on this chair, a lady's petticoat and vest. On the mantelpiece: a clock and candelabra; to the right, a tray with a carafe of water and an upturned glass on top; to the left, a spirit lamp and a box of matches. Right of the hall door, a sofa against the wall. In the corner, a small table, placed at an angle. A woman's dressing gown thrown across the foot of the bed. YVONNE's heel-less slippers on the floor, downstage of the bed: LUCIEN's slippers on the other side. In the ceiling, a chandelier, operated by a switch on the left of the hall door.

When the curtain rises, the stage is in semi-darkness, lit only by the nightlight next to the bed. YVONNE is in bed, sleeping deeply: her light, regular breathing can be heard. Five seconds after the curtain has risen, the front door bell rings, off. This does not wake YVONNE but slightly disturbs her: she utters a long sigh and stirs under the sheets. Ten seconds after the first ring, the bell rings again. YVONNE, who is sleeping on the left side of the bed, opens her eyes, which are swollen with sleep, and raises her head.

YVONNE: What on earth's that?
    (*The bell rings again.*)
    (*Angrily.*) I suppose that's Lucien! Forgotten his key!
    (*Throwing back the bedclothes.*) It's ridiculous, scaring the life out of you like this! (*She jumps out of bed, wearing a nightdress.*)
    (*The bell rings again, twice.*)

(*Furious.*) Coming! (*She snatches up her dressing gown and quickly slides her feet into her slippers.*)

(*The bell rings repeatedly.*)

YVONNE: I said I'm coming! (*Not having time to put on her dressing gown, she throws it round her neck like a scarf. She then goes into the hall, to the front door of the flat. Roughly.*) Who's there?

LUCIEN: (*Off, woefully, like a naughty child, frightened of being scolded.*) It's me... I've forgotten my key.

YVONNE: (*In the hall.*) Oh! Naturally! (*She opens the door; the noise of the lock can be heard.*) Just what I needed! (*She comes back into the room and moves downstage.*) Come along! Come on in!

(*Arriving downstage right, she climbs into bed on her knees, with her back to the audience. While she is doing this, LUCIEN has closed the front door and can be heard fixing the safety chain. As YVONNE says "Come in", he appears. He is wearing a Louis XIV costume under a raincoat, buttoned up to the top and only coming down to his buttocks. The collar is turned up and a scarf tied round his neck. His white gloves are soaking wet. His shoes are covered with mud and so are his stockings, up to the calf. The back of his raincoat is one large, wet stain. When he enters, he has his hands tangled up with a lighted candle, his Louis XIV cane and his umbrella. His sword catches in the door, as he comes through.*)

YVONNE: (*In bed.*) Well? What are you waiting for? Tomorrow?

LUCIEN: Here I am!... I'm sorry. (*He switches on the chandelier.*)

YVONNE: (*Angrily.*) You're sorry! Why can't you remember your key? Do you think I like being jolted awake when I'm fast asleep?

LUCIEN: (*Embarrassed.*) I woke you?

YVONNE: (*Icily.*) Of course you woke me! You don't think I waited up for you till this hour?

LUCIEN: (*Very sincerely, as if relieved, as he turns towards the mantelpiece to put down his candle.*) Oh! Good!

(*He is about to blow out the candle, but stops at the sound of YVONNE's voice.*)

YVONNE: Good! You're glad you woke me?

LUCIEN: No! I meant good... because you hadn't waited up.

(*He blows out his candle, puts it on the mantelpiece, stands his cane in the corner of the fireplace and then, with his umbrella under his arm, half open and dripping water, goes towards the bed, shaking his frozen hands in his wet gloves.*)

YVONNE: Really! What a time to come home!

LUCIEN: (*Taking off his gloves.*) I couldn't find a cab. And the weather! The only buses were going in the opposite direction. There's never a bus going the right way!

YVONNE: I can't think what time it is!

LUCIEN: (*Without conviction.*) Oh no, it's hardly...

(*At this precise moment the clock on the mantelpiece begins to strike four.*)

YVONNE: (*Cutting him short.*) Wait!

(*They both listen, LUCIEN with a wry face.*)

YVONNE: (*Tight-lipped.*) Ten past four.

LUCIEN: Ten past?

YVONNE: (*Sharply.*) Of course! The clock's ten minutes slow.

LUCIEN: It can't be, it must be wrong. Just now when I passed the Gare St Lazare...

YVONNE: Yes, yes, I know! It was midnight!

LUCIEN: Midnight, no, but...

YVONNE: Yes, yes! It's a well-known fact. When husbands start sleeping in other beds, their wives' clocks are always wrong.

LUCIEN: (*Going to the bed.*) Oh! You're exaggerating! I'm sleeping in other beds now! (*Sitting on the foot of the bed.*) It was agreed I'd be home late, as I was going to the Four Arts Ball. I couldn't leave before it started...

YVONNE: (*Irrefutably.*) You shouldn't have gone in the first place! It's not meant for you! What they must have thought of you at the Four Arts... You, a married man!

LUCIEN: (*Who has still not put down his umbrella, tracing designs with it on the carpet, as if with a stick in sand.*) Oh, nobody bothered about me!

YVONNE: (*Suddenly giving him a blow in the buttocks with her knee underneath the bedclothes.*) Do be careful!

LUCIEN: (*Leaping off the bed.*) What?

YVONNE: (*Shouting.*) Your umbrella! You're flooding the carpet!

LUCIEN: Me! (*Instinctively he lowers his head to assess the damage, so that a stream of water escapes from the brim of his hat.*)

YVONNE: (*Shouting louder.*) And your hat!... It's pouring water!

LUCIEN: (*Completely stunned, rushing towards the door, to put his hat and umbrella in the hall.*) Oh!... I'm sorry!

YVONNE: Can't you see the brim's full?

LUCIEN: (*Going out.*) Brimful! I wish I was!

YVONNE: (*Raging.*) Oh, yes! Be witty!

(*LUCIEN has re-entered and stopped woefully between the door and the bureau. He pulls clumsily at one end of his scarf, to get it out of his raincoat collar. YVONNE looks at him pityingly.*)

Oh! Just look at yourself!

LUCIEN: It's the rain!

YVONNE: A fine sight! Look at those stockings!

LUCIEN: (*Woefully.*) They are rather muddy!

YVONNE: Rather muddy! Oh!!!... (*Sharply.*) Take off your coat! You're not going to bed in it, are you?

LUCIEN: (*Having decided to make every concession.*) Quite right!

(*He turns his back to the audience and takes off his coat, which he puts on the chair at the right of the door. Then he draws his sword with a broad sweep of his arm and stands it up against the mantelpiece.*)

YVONNE: I must say!

(*LUCIEN has come back downstage centre and shivers.*) (*Nagging.*) What's the matter?

LUCIEN: (*Indicating with his head that it's nothing; then.*) I'm cold!

YVONNE: (*Sarcastically.*) You're cold! I suppose you want me to feel sorry for you!

LUCIEN: (*With signs of impatience.*) No. You asked me, so
I told you.

YVONNE: That will teach you to go out enjoying yourself!... (*Pityingly.*) What are you doing in the fireplace?

LUCIEN: (*Still at the fireplace, very simply.*) I'm trying to get
warm.

YVONNE: There's no fire!

LUCIEN: (*Repeating automatically.*) There's no... eh?
(*Casting a look at the grate.*) Oh! Yes... habit, you know!
When there is a fire, I put my... so, without thinking...

YVONNE: Pah!

LUCIEN: (*Pathetically.*) You're not very charitable,
destroying my illusions. I was starting to get warm!

YVONNE: Your illusions keep you warm, do they? Well,
in future... when you want a fire...

LUCIEN: (*Irritated, shrugging his shoulders as he goes upstage.*)
Oh... Rubbish!

YVONNE: (*Returning to the charge.*) We've only been
married two years and you abandon me to go to the Four
Arts Ball!

LUCIEN: Now listen! I'm tired, you can make a scene
tomorrow!

YVONNE: Oh!... I'll have you know I'm not making a scene!

LUCIEN: (*Coming downstage a little.*) Can't you understand, if a man's not going to turn into a fossil, he
must see everything, know everything... to form his
mind...

YVONNE: (*With the utmost scorn.*) Oh, no!... No! Just listen
to him! You're a cashier at the Galeries Lafayette.
What do you have to know about the Four Arts Ball?

LUCIEN: (*Offended.*) I'm not only a cashier. I'm a painter.

YVONNE: (*Shrugging her shoulders.*) A painter! Those daubs!

LUCIEN: (*Annoyed.*) Daubs!

YVONNE: Precisely! If you don't sell them, they're
daubs. Have you ever sold one?

LUCIEN: No, I haven't. Of course I haven't. It's unkind
to say that. I haven't sold one... because nobody's
bought one... otherwise...

YVONNE: You've only once painted anything successfully.

LUCIEN: (*Happy with this concession.*) Ah!

YVONNE: My bath!

LUCIEN: (*Annoyed, reaching the fireplace.*) Oh! Very funny! Very witty! Carry on! (*Coming back towards the bed.*) I'm a better artist than you think. So, as an artist, it's only natural I should look for artistic excitement.

YVONNE: All right! Say you're looking for excitement! But don't talk about art!

LUCIEN: (*Giving up the possibility of arguing.*) Oh! You're just attacking me. (*He goes to the fireplace and stands in front of the mirror, about to take off his jabot.*)

YVONNE: No! (*She jumps out of bed, then runs barefooted to LUCIEN and turns him round to face her.*) If I'm attacking you, give me one example! One example of your artistic excitement!

LUCIEN: Yes, definitely!

YVONNE: (*Icily.*) That's no answer! Give me an example! (*She comes back downstage.*)

LUCIEN: (*Coming downstage after her.*) There were lots... For instance, the entrance of Amphitrite. (*Looking at her with a slightly scornful smile.*) You've probably never heard of Amphitrite.

YVONNE: Oh, haven't I? I've never heard of Amphitrite! It's a stomach disease.

LUCIEN: (*Dumbfounded.*) What?

YVONNE: Precisely!

LUCIEN: (*Bursting out laughing.*) A stomach disease! She's the goddess of the sea.

YVONNE: (*Taken aback.*) Oh?... (*Bad-tempered.*) I confused her with enteritis.

LUCIEN: They're totally different.

YVONNE: Anyone can make a mistake.

LUCIEN: Yes. Well, when the procession made its entrance, that was an artistic excitement. A superb model, completely naked, in a shell of mother-of-pearl, borne by tritons and sirens!

YVONNE: (*Stiffly.*) A woman completely naked!

LUCIEN: Completely naked!

YVONNE: Very proper!

LUCIEN: (*Very deliberately.*), That's precisely where you're wrong. There was nothing improper about it.

YVONNE: Yes? Well, I'll do the same... (*As she speaks,she arrives downstage right and climbs into bed.*)

LUCIEN: (*Raising his arms to heaven.*) For heavens sake!... That's a ridiculous thing to say!

YVONNE: (*In bed, squatting.*) Why? Either a thing's improper or it isn't.

LUCIEN: It isn't when it's a model... And this one!... What a figure!... And her breasts, ah... I've never seen such breasts! (*He goes to the fireplace.*)

YVONNE: (*Acknowledging with a nod: then, stiffly.*) Thank you very much!

LUCIEN: (*Turning round, taken aback.*) What?

YVONNE: How very polite!

LUCIEN: (*After raising his eyes to heaven.*) All right, you want to take offence again. I wasn't referring to you. Of course yours are very pretty... but they're not the breasts of a model! (*He turns round to the mirror to undo his jabot.*)

YVONNE: Oh, really? (*She throws back the bedclothes and jumps out of bed to rush at LUCIEN, hurriedly undoing the ribbons of her nightdress.*) Well... well... (*When she reaches him, she turns him round to face her.*) What's wrong with them? (*Facing him, with her back to the audience, she plants herself in front of him, the front of her nightdress open and held wide apart with both hands.*)

LUCIEN: (*Completely dumbfounded.*) Eh? I don't know... Well, there, for instance... (*He points.*)

YVONNE: (*Slapping his hand and leaning back.*) No! Don't touch me! Go and touch hers, as they're better than mine!

LUCIEN: Oh! Don't be silly!

YVONNE: (*Returning to the charge.*) Go on, tell me! What's wrong with them?

LUCIEN: (*Confined between the right edge of the lefthand door frame and YVONNE who is close up to him.*) Oh!

Practically nothing!... Underneath they're fine!
You see I'm being fair. But on top, well, they're slightly concave.

YVONNE: (*Indignant.*) Concave!

LUCIEN: (*Illustrating it with a gesture.*) Which makes them rather like coathooks.

YVONNE: (*Quickly tying up the ribbons of her nightdress.*) Coathooks! That's too much! (*She seizes him by the left arm and sends him whirling to the centre of the stage.*)

LUCIEN: (*Not knowing what's happened to him.*) Oh! What is it?

YVONNE: (*Having opened the door, which she has thus cleared, calling.*) Annette!... Annette!

ANNETTE: (*Off, sleepily.*) Mm?

YVONNE: Annette! Get up!

LUCIEN: (*Surprised.*) Annette?

YVONNE: Did you hear what I said?

ANNETTE: (*Off.*) Eh?

YVONNE: Come along! On your feet!

ANNETTE: (*Off.*) All right!

LUCIEN: Annette? Annette's in my room?

YVONNE: (*Passing in front of him to go and sit on the stool at the foot of the bed.*) Yes, of course she is!

LUCIEN: This is too much! You make the maid sleep in my bed?

YVONNE: Perhaps you'd rather I stayed in the flat alone, while you're out on the town enjoying yourself? No, thank you very much! (*Leaning her left arm on the iron rail at the foot of the bed.*) I'd be too frightened.

LUCIEN: This is the limit! The maid in my bed! Where am I going to sleep?

YVONNE: Well... There! (*She points to the door, left.*)

LUCIEN: With the maid?

YVONNE: The maid, the maid! Now you're home, Annette will go up to her room and you'll have your own bed.

LUCIEN: Certainly not. In her sheets!

YVONNE: They're not her sheets, they're yours.

LUCIEN: She's slept in them, that's enough for me!

YVONNE: (*Rising and climbing into bed.*) Oh, of course! If you had to sleep in the sheets of a completely naked model, you wouldn't be in the least disgusted...

LUCIEN: (*Rather excited at the thought.*) Mm!

YVONNE: (*On her knees on the bed, busily shaking the pillows as she talks, and turning round towards him.*) What did I say? (*Moving on her knees to the middle of the bed.*) You'd prefer that, wouldn't you? (*Continuing to the end of the bed.*) You'd prefer that, say so... you beast! (*She lies down again in bed.*)

LUCIEN: (*Losing all patience.*) Oh!!!... Shut up! (*He reaches the fireplace.*)

(*ANNETTE enters left. She is wearing a coarse linen nightdress, gathered and cut low across the chest and back, with short flared sleeves coming down to her biceps: a woollen petticoat underneath, hanging below it. Her bare legs are in felt slippers. Her hair is untidy, in bandeaux at the front and in two tight pigtails, sticking up in the air, at the back. She comes forward, only half awake, her eyes swollen with sleep.*)

YVONNE: (*Jumping out of bed and running towards her.*) Come here! Do you know what he said?

ANNETTE: (*Yawning.*) No.

YVONNE: He said I've breasts like coathooks.

ANNETTE: (*Not caring, half asleep.*) Oh?... Very good, Madame.

LUCIEN: (*Sarcastically.*) You got the maid up to tell her that?

YVONNE: Precisely! I want her to say what she thinks about my breasts, to show you everybody doesn't share your opinion. (*To Annette.*) What did you say about them the other morning?

ANNETTE: (*Painfully opening her eyes.*) I don't know.

YVONNE: (*Emphasising each part of her sentences with a tap on Annette's arm or chest.*) Of course you do! When I was getting dressed, I said "Look, there aren't many women with breasts as firm as that". And what did you say?

ANNETTE: (*Making an effort.*) Ah, yes! I said "That's right. Next to them, mine look like old sacks."

YVONNE: There! You hear?

LUCIEN: (*Seizing Annette sharply by the arm and making her pass across.*) All right! What does that prove? I've never denied you've a rare bosom. But there's still a margin between the rare and the unique.

(*ANNETTE, waiting for them to end their argument, has sat down on the chair near the fireplace and begun to doze off.*)

YVONNE: Really? Well, from now on, you can say goodbye to my bosom.

LUCIEN: (*Putting his hand forward to answer.*) Now look...

YVONNE: (*Misunderstanding his gesture and slapping his hand.*) Hands off!

LUCIEN: (*Furious.*) For heavens sake!

YVONNE: I'll keep it for others... who can appreciate it. (*She has come downstage right and climbs into bed.*)

LUCIEN: (*Furious, walking up and down, his hands in his trouser pockets.*) Fine! Keep it for others! Keep it for anyone you like! The Pope, if you want to! Oh!!! You need the patience of a... (*Without looking, he collapses into the chair where Annette is dozing.*)

ANNETTE: (*Woken up with a start and yelling.*) Oh!

LUCIEN: (*Jumping up, furious.*) Oh! Go to bed!

ANNETTE: (*Grumbling, as she goes upstage.*) Is this why you got me up?

LUCIEN: (*Upstage of bed.*) I didn't get you up. My wife did.

ANNETTE: You could just as well have let me go on sleeping.

YVONNE: All right, Annette! Nobody asked for your opinion.

(*ANNETTE was going out, but stops at the sound of YVONNE's voice.*)

As you're up, you can go to your own room and give that one back to my husband.

(*ANNETTE once again goes towards the door, but stops as before, this time at the sound of LUCIEN's voice.*)

LUCIEN: (*Peremptorily.*) No! No! She's got it, she can keep it. I'll sleep here.

YVONNE: With me? Oh, no!

LUCIEN: (*As before.*) All right! You can sleep where you like. This is our bed, I've a right to sleep in it.

YVONNE: Very well! But if you're hoping for anything, you're making a big mistake.

LUCIEN: (*Shrugging his shoulders.*) I'm not hoping for anything. (*He goes upstage of the bed and, with his back to the audience, sits down and begins to take off his shoes.*)

YVONNE: (*Rearranging the bedclothes.*) I'm glad to hear it.

LUCIEN: (*Sharply to Annette, who is asleep on her feet against the doorframe, left.*) Get to bed, you!

ANNETTE: (*The victim.*) Yes, sir.

LUCIEN: Go on, Mona Lisa, go on!

ANNETTE: What a hole!

(*ANNETTE goes out, shrugging her shoulders.*)

YVONNE: It's too much! Going off and getting excited about another woman and then making do with me! I'm no understudy.

LUCIEN: (*Fed up.*) Now please! You can tell me in the morning. I'm tired.

YVONNE: (*Burying herself in the bedclothes with her back to him.*) You're right! Instead of arguing, I'd do better to get some sleep.

LUCIEN: That's it. Go to sleep!

(*A pause.*)

YVONNE: (*Half sitting up and talking over her shoulder.*) I Must say, I'm glad the maid settled your nonsense!

LUCIEN: (*Standing up, furious and pointing to the door with a slipper.*) Listen!... Do you want me to go?

YVONNE: (*With her head on the pillow, completely unconcerned.*) Go, if you like!

LUCIEN: (*Exasperated, hobbling up and down with one foot in a slipper.*) Oh! Oh! Oh! (*Coming back to the foot of the bed.*) In the first place, what does the maid know? (*Putting on his other slipper, without sitting down.*) obviously if she's only got her breasts to compare them with, I agree that between hers and...

YVONNE: (*Jumping up to a sitting position.*) Oh! You want a more expert opinion? All right! Tomorrow the head of the scent department at the Galeries Lafayette is coming to dinner. And Monsieur Bonhomme. I'll show them my bosom. They can say what they think of it.

LUCIEN: (*Scandalized.*) You must be mad!

YVONNE: Why? You've just said it's not improper.

LUCIEN: (*Forcefully.*) It's not improper if you're completely naked.

YVONNE: (*Quickly.*) Then I'll be completely naked.

LUCIEN: (*Dumbfounded.*) She's mad! Completely mad!

YVONNE: (*Quietly, as she buries herself under the bedclothes again.*) Breasts like coathooks, have I? We'll see about that!

LUCIEN: (*Going to the foot of the bed, his hands clasped.*) Now, please stop! Please!

YVONNE: (*Raising herself half up: scornfully.*) Well... Go to bed! What are you waiting for? You're not going to stay dressed up as the Sun King all night?

LUCIEN: (*Faintly, tapping his stomach gently with his finger-tips.*) No.

YVONNE: (*Looking at him pityingly, nagging.*) What's the matter now?

LUCIEN: (*Wretched.*) I've a stomach ache.

YVONNE: Marvellous! Something else! (*She throws back the bedclothes and jumps out of bed.*)

LUCIEN: I wish Annette would make me some camomile tea!

YVONNE: (*Putting on her slippers.*) All right! You can have your camomile tea! (*She goes towards the door, left.*)

LUCIEN: (*Standing in her way.*) Who asked you to get up? I can do it.

YVONNE: (*Pushing him away.*) Oh, no! No! (*Coming back to him.*) I'm not going to have you saying I let you die. No!... I know my duty... And I do it!

LUCIEN: (*In the same tone as YVONNE.*) Good! Fine! I'm glad to hear it. (*He goes and sits on the stool.*)

YVONNE: (*Going to the door, left, and calling.*) Annette!

ANNETTE: (*Off, fed up.*) Oh!!!

YVONNE: Annette! Get up!

ANNETTE: (*Off.*) What! Again!

YVONNE: "Again"! Yes, again! What do you mean, again? Make my husband some camomile tea! (*She goes to the mantelpiece and strikes a match to light the spirit lamp.*) (*ANNETTE can be heard grumbling. A pause.*)

LUCIEN: (*With a scornful laugh.*) The way you pester that girl!

YVONNE: (*Turning round, the match box in one hand, a match in the other.*) What? That's the limit! I'm pestering her? (*Going to him and speaking straight into his face.*) Now listen! Is the camomile tea for me? Eh? Is it for me?

LUCIEN: (*Almost shouting.*) My supper's lying on my stomach!

YVONNE: (*At the same pitch as LUCIEN.*) Yes, it always does! (*Going back to the mantelpiece to make the tea: lighting the lamp and pouring water from the carafe into the saucepan.*) This is what he comes home with! Indigestion from gallivanting round the town! His wife's not good enough for his evening's entertainment, but quite good enough to be his sick nurse!
(*LUCIEN has not been listening to this diatribe, thinking only about his stomach ache. He struggles against it, tapping the pit of his stomach with his finger tips. He then rises and comes up behind her.*)

LUCIEN: Darling?

YVONNE: (*Curtly, without turning round.*) What?

LUCIEN: Is it nearly ready?

YVONNE: Give it time!... It has to boil first!... You know that!

LUCIEN: (*Resigned.*) Yes. (*A pause, hiccups, in pain.*) Oh!

YVONNE: (*Turning half round.*) What?

LUCIEN: (*Leaning on her; plaintively.*) I want to be sick!

YVONNE: (*Pushing him sharply away and moving across.*) Oh, no! No! You're not going to be sick! I didn't marry you for that!

LUCIEN: No, no! I said I want to, not I'm going to. You know I never can.

YVONNE: (*With contempt.*) Yes, I know!... Very sad! (*She goes back to the bed and climbs into it.*)
(*ANNETTE enters, carrying a packet of camomile and a bowl of sugar. She has put on a white dressing jacket and stockings, which are falling down over her ankles.*)

ANNETTE: (*Sulkily as she puts the camomile in the boiling water.*) Nothing else you want, while I'm here?

YVONNE: (*In bed, arranging the bedclothes round her.*) Ask him, Annette! He's the one who's ill.

LUCIEN: (*Exhausted.*) I've stomach ache.

ANNETTE: (*As before, without turning round.*) If he didn't go out all night...

LUCIEN: (*Getting angry.*) Oh, no! No! Don't you start!

ANNETTE: (*Unconcerned.*) I only meant...

LUCIEN: Yes, all right! Go to bed!

ANNETTE: (*Not needing to be told twice.*) I'd be glad to.

LUCIEN: (*To YVONNE.*) Oh, no...

ANNETTE: (*Thinking he is talking to her.*) Oh, yes!

LUCIEN: (*Furious.*) I'm talking to my wife!

ANNETTE: Oh!
(*ANNETTE goes out.*)

LUCIEN: No! I'm not having the servants interfering too!

YVONNE: (*With a wry smile.*) I can't think why you got angry with her. She's right. If you hadn't had supper...

LUCIEN: That may be. But it's no business of hers. If I have to start explaining to her...! (*He sits on the stool.*) I had supper because I was hungry... And because I was with Monsieur Bonhomme and the Spink brothers; they suggested having something to eat. Is that a crime?

YVONNE: No, it's not a crime. Of course it isn't. But it's silly eating so much, you get indigestion. Having to have supper!...
(*A long pause.*)
(*Icily and scornfully.*) Who paid?

LUCIEN: (*Shrugging his shoulders.*) Nobody.

YVONNE: What do you mean, nobody?

LUCIEN: Well, everybody. Their own share.

YVONNE: I'm surprised it wasn't you. Showing off as usual!

LUCIEN: Me!

YVONNE: Yes, you! You're a miser in your own home. But as soon as there's anyone else around... megalomania!

LUCIEN: (*Rising and going upstage in a circular movement.*) I've megalomania! Marvellous! I've megalomania!

YVONNE: (*Going straight on, as he stops.*) I only have to look at you. I only have to look at you! What do you dress up as? The Sun King! I ask you! The Sun King!... In a thunderstorm! It's ridiculous!

LUCIEN: (*Sitting on the chair next to the bureau.*) You're the one who's mad!

YVONNE: (*Not giving in.*) You love strutting about as Louis the Fifteenth!

LUCIEN: (*After looking at her in scornful mockery, shrugs his shoulders: then, unconcerned.*) Fourteenth.

YVONNE: Fourteenth what?

LUCIEN: The Sun King was Louis the Fourteenth.

YVONNE: (*Taken aback.*) Oh?... (*Getting angry.*) All right, Louis the Fourteenth! (*Sharply.*) That's typical of you! Arguing with me about a Louis, but when it comes to your pleasures, you never think twice!

LUCIEN: (*Rising and, in a semi-circular movement reaching the stool, where he sits down.*) Oh, exquisite! Charming! Delightful!

(*A pause.*)

YVONNE: (*In the same icy tone.*) What did you spend on your supper?

LUCIEN: (*With an impatient gesture.*) How do I know?

YVONNE: (*Shrugging her shoulders, then, kneeling on the bed.*) You don't even know what you spent?

LUCIEN: (*After raising his eyes to heaven.*) Eleven francs seventy five. There!

YVONNE: (*Rising to her full height on her knees, with her hands gripping the rail at the foot of the bed, emphasising every syllable.*) Eleven francs seventy five for a bite of food!... There! What did I say? (*Changing her tone.*) The other day...

LUCIEN: (*Feeling the scene is going to move onto new ground and excitedly shaking his head: then, raising his eyes to heaven, quietly to himself.*) Oh, God! (*He moves upstage.*)

YVONNE: (*Not giving up, jumping off the bed: between her teeth.*) You brute! (*She runs upstage to him and turns him round by the arm to make him face her.*) The other day when I bought a bottle of scent, you said I'd ruined you. And you spend...(*Emphasising.*) ...eleven francs seventy five on your supper! At least I've still got my scent, I'm using it! But where's your supper now?

LUCIEN: (*Furious, hitting himself in the stomach.*) Here! Here!

YVONNE: (*Releasing him, then going back to the bed and climbing into it.*) A lot of good that's done you! A pity you didn't keep your eleven francs seventy five... to pay for the curtains!

LUCIEN: (*Having sat down on the chair next to the bureau.*) They cost eight hundred. You can't see me offering eleven seventy five!

YVONNE: At least you'd have shown willing. I only mention them, because the man came today.

LUCIEN: (*Pricking up his ears.*) Oh?

YVONNE: He said he was fed up with being put off. If you don't pay him something substantial on account, he'll issue a writ. And send it to the Galeries Lafayette. You can imagine the impression that will make!

LUCIEN: (*Rising and coming downstage.*) He said that?

YVONNE: Yes.

LUCIEN: This is blackmail! (*Towards the hall door, as if speaking to the man.*) Very well, sir... (*To her.*) I was thinking of paying him something...

YVONNE: (*Implacable.*) When?

LUCIEN: (*Taken aback.*) Hm!... When I can! But as it is! He can whistle for it.

YVONNE: (*Hammering each syllable, raising her hands to heaven.*) Yet you go and spend eleven francs seventy five on your supper!

LUCIEN: (*Having gone upstage beyond the bed, losing his temper.*) Will you shut up about my supper!

YVONNE: (*Not letting up.*) If I were you, it would be lying on my stomach.

LUCIEN: (*Straight into her face.*) It is, dammit, it is!

YVONNE: (*Shouting as loudly as him.*) Don't shout like that!... For the last hour you've been tiring me out with your arguing!

LUCIEN: (*Coming downstage.*) That's the limit! I'm arguing! I'm wearing you out!

YVONNE: Don't you want to get some sleep?

LUCIEN: (*Coming back upstage of the bed.*) Oh, yes! Sleep! Sleep! I'm exhausted!

YVONNE: (*Turning her back on him and burying herself under the bedclothes.*) All right, then! So am I! Goodnight!

LUCIEN: (*In the same tone.*) Goodnight!

YVONNE: And shut up!

LUCIEN: (*Sitting down on the end of the bed.*) And shut up!

YVONNE: (*Kicking him under the bedclothes, as he's sat on her ankle.*) My foot!

LUCIEN: (*Furious.*) Oh! Your foot! (*Putting his left foot on the rail at the end of the bed, to get his knee level with his hand, so he can undo the garter at the bottom of his knee breeches.*) Ah! Bed! (*He undoes the garter.*) A cannon ball wouldn't get me out of it!

(*A pause. Suddenly the front door bell rings in the hall. They remain for a moment without moving, as if bewitched. The bell rings again. YVONNE slowly lifts her head and, rising to a sitting position, looks anxiously at LUCIEN. He takes his foot slowly off the rail and, turning completely round to his left, looks questioningly at YVONNE.*)

YVONNE: (*Choked voice.*) What on earth is that?

LUCIEN: (*Same voice.*) I don't know... It's the front door.
(*The bell rings again, making them jump.*)

YVONNE: (*With a start.*) Oh, heavens!

LUCIEN: It can't be a visitor.

YVONNE: At this hour it must be something serious.

LUCIEN: (*Panic-stricken.*) Yes.

(*The bell rings again.*)

YVONNE: (*Jumping out of bed and putting on her slippers.*) Again! Oh, Lucien, Lucien, I'm frightened! (*She snatches up her dressing gown from the foot of the bed.*)

LUCIEN: (*As worried as she is.*) Now, now! Be brave, dammit! Don't let yourself get upset!

YVONNE: (*Panic-stricken, going from right to left as if not knowing what she's looking for.*) It's easy for you to talk. You're a man, but I...

(*The bell rings again.*)

Oh!

LUCIEN: (*Turning round and round in the same place.*) What can it be? What can it be?

YVONNE: Where, where, where?

LUCIEN: Where's who?

YVONNE: (*Waving her arms wildly.*) My dressing gown? Where have I put my dressing gown?

LUCIEN: It's in your hand.

YVONNE: Oh! Yes!

(*The bell rings repeatedly.*)

LUCIEN and YVONNE: Oh!

YVONNE: (*Trying in vain to put on her dressing gown.*) Oh! This ringing's driving me mad!

LUCIEN: (*Pointing to the door, left.*) And Annette there! Not moving!

(*He runs towards her door.*)

YVONNE: (*Giving up trying to put on her dressing gown and running to join him.*) Oh! That girl!

LUCIEN and YVONNE: (*In the doorway, he upstage.*) Annette! Annette!

ANNETTE: (*Off.*) Mm?

YVONNE: Quick! Get up!

ANNETTE: (*Off.*) Eh? Again?

(*The bell rings again.*)

YVONNE: Do hurry!

LUCIEN: Can't you hear the bell?

ANNETTE: (*Off, tearful.*) Oh!!! They're trying to kill me!

YVONNE: (*Going upstage of the stool.*) I hope nothing's happened to the family.

LUCIEN: (*Near the fireplace.*) No, no! You'll end up terrifying both of us.

YVONNE: (*Quickly putting her dressing gown down on the bed, seeing the stool and tapping it.*) Oh! Touch wood! Touch wood!

LUCIEN: Of course if something really...

YVONNE: Touch wood, I tell you!

LUCIEN: (*Confused.*) Yes. Of course if something...

YVONNE: Go on, touch wood!

LUCIEN: Yes. (*Without knowing what he is doing, he touches three times the marble mantelpiece which is within reach.*)

YVONNE: Not that, it's marble!

LUCIEN: Oh, you're confusing me. (*He goes and touches the bureau.*)

YVONNE: With the palm of your hand! The palm!

LUCIEN: (*Obeying automatically.*) The palm!

YVONNE: Oh! You'll bring us bad luck.
  (*Prolonged ringing of the bell.*)
  (*Rushing towards the door, left.*) What is that girl doing?

LUCIEN: (*Following her.*) Get a move on there!
  (*ANNETTE enters. They each seize her by an arm and push her forward in front of them. She tries to go back, but each time they push her forward towards the hall door, so that she is almost spinning like a teetotum.*)

ANNETTE: (*With tears of rage.*) Oh! No! I've had enough! Give me my wages, I want to go!

YVONNE: (*Her patience exhausted.*) Yes, yes. Fine! go!

LUCIEN: (*Also impatient.*) Go on.
  (*The next five lines are almost simultaneous.*)

ANNETTE: Working all night! You're killing me!
  (*The bell rings.*)

LUCIEN: Will you open the door, you fool!

YVONNE: Go on, go on!

ANNETTE: (*Pushed towards the hall door.*) Yes, but pay me my wages!

LUCIEN: Oh! This girl! This girl!

(*ANNETTE has now gone out into the hall. LUCIEN is on the right of the hall door, YVONNE on the left.*)

ANNETTE: (*Off.*) Who is it out there?

JOSEPH: (*Off, in the distance.*) Joseph, Madame's mother's new servant.

YVONNE: (*Shrilly.*) Mother! Something's happened to mother! Something's happened to mother!

LUCIEN: Don't shout like that! Don't shout like that!

(*During the last two lines, the safety chain could be heard being drawn back and the front door opened. JOSEPH enters. He is wearing evening dress trousers and waist-coat with an ordinary jacket. He has a woollen scarf round his neck and is carrying a bowler hat. As soon as he enters, YVONNE seizes him and comes downstage to the footlights. ANNETTE closes the front door and promptly re-enters, coming downstage near the fireplace.*)

YVONNE: (*Not giving JOSEPH time to speak.*) What's happened to mother? What's happened to mother?

JOSEPH: (*Very embarrassed, his head lowered.*) Well, you see...

(*In his embarrassment he turns his head towards LUCIEN, not having had time to see him, when he entered. His eyes fall on LUCIEN's legs and travel up the length of his body with surprise. He is unable to suppress a cry of amazement at the sight of this man dressed as Louis XIV.*)

Oh!

LUCIEN: (*Instinctively looking at his own costume.*) What? What's the matter? Go on, tell me, don't stare at my costume! There's nothing extraordinary about that.

YVONNE: (*To JOSEPH.*) An accident?

LUCIEN: (*His head lowered, automatically twisting his hat in his hands: quickly.*) Oh, no...

YVONNE: (*Breathing.*) Ah!

LUCIEN: There, you see, no accident!

JOSEPH: (*As before, but hesitant.*) But... she's not very well...

YVONNE: (*Distressed.*) Mother's not well? What's the matter?

JOSEPH: (*As before.*) Well... she's ill.

YVONNE: (*Hardly daring to ask questions.*) Oh!... Very?

JOSEPH: (*As before.*) Well... rather!

YVONNE: (*Moving across to seek refuge in LUCIEN's arms.*) Lucien!... Lucien!... Mother's ill!

LUCIEN: Come now!

YVONNE: Mother's very ill!

LUCIEN: There, there!

JOSEPH: (*As before.*) When I say very ill, that's a matter of speaking, because the fact is she's actually... actually...

YVONNE: (*A lump in her throat.*) What, what? She's actually what?

JOSEPH: She's actually... (*Raising his head: very abruptly.*) dead!

LUCIEN *and* YVONNE: Oh!
(*YVONNE faints. LUCIEN catches her.*)

LUCIEN: (*Sitting down quickly on the floor, still holding her.*) Oh! I thought this would happen!

JOSEPH: You see... they suggested I should break the news gently, so I shouldn't upset her too much. (*Aside, with a long sigh of relief.*) Phew!

LUCIEN: What a disaster! Just when we were going to bed!

ANNETTE: (*Very upset.*) Oh dear! Oh dear!

LUCIEN: Oh! Why did you have to come here?

JOSEPH: I was told to!

LUCIEN: You were told to? Told to!... All right! Give me a hand!

JOSEPH: Yes, sir. (*He puts his hat on the bureau and kneels behind YVONNE.*)
(*LUCIEN hands YVONNE to JOSEPH and comes slightly downstage between her and the stool.*)

ANNETTE: (*Near the fireplace.*) Oh dear! Oh dear!
(*LUCIEN steps over YVONNE and goes to ANNETTE. He then pushes her towards the door, left.*)

LUCIEN: You go and get some vinegar or salts, instead of shouting "Oh dear, oh dear." That doesn't help.

ANNETTE: Yes, sir. (*As she goes out.*) Oh dear, oh dear!
　(*ANNETTE goes out. In the meantime, to hold YVONNE,
　JOSEPH has passed his forearms under her armpits and
　put his hands against her chest, so that he is in effect holding
　her breasts in his cupped hands.*)

JOSEPH: Let's put her... on the bed!
　(*JOSEPH emphasises each syllable of "on the bed", by moving
　his hands in the direction of the bed, thus shaking YVONNE's
　breasts each time he does so.*)

LUCIEN: (*Coming back to him.*) Eh? Yes... (*Seeing what he is
　doing and rushing to him.*) What are you doing there?

JOSEPH: (*Still holding her with both hands and shaking her
　gently.*) Holding her.

LUCIEN: (*Trying to push him aside, so that he can take his
　place.*) Don't hold her like that! Can't you see she's not
　wearing a corset?

JOSEPH: (*Without letting go.*) Oh! You can't believe I think
　about that sort of thing!

LUCIEN: (*As before, now on his knees, left of YVONNE.*) I
　don't give a damn what you think or don't think! I tell
　you to let go of her! (*He pushes him away upstage and,
　still on his knees, moves to YVONNE's right.*) Look and see
　if there isn't some ether in that bottle next to the bed!

JOSEPH: (*Rushing upstage of the bed to look.*) Yes, sir. Yes.

LUCIEN: (*Grumbling.*) Fondling her like that! (*Seeing
　JOSEPH upstage of the bed.*) Not there! On the table,
　look! Next to the bed!

JOSEPH: Yes, sir, yes! (*He vaults over the bed to reach the other
　side.*)

LUCIEN: Oh! The sheets! The sheets!

JOSEPH: (*Having uncorked the bottle and smelt the contents.*)
　This is it, sir.

LUCIEN: Good. Give it here.
　(*JOSEPH runs to him with it.*)
　Yvonne! Yvonne darling! Yvonne! (*To JOSEPH.*) A
　towel! Find me a towel, so I can dab her forehead!

JOSEPH: (*Not knowing which way to turn and swivelling
　round to left and right on the same spot like a weathercock.*)
　A towel? Where's a towel?

LUCIEN: (*Uncorking the bottle with his teeth.*) I don't know. If I did, I wouldn't ask you. Have a look!

JOSEPH: (*Seeing YVONNE's vest on the left hand chair and running across her legs to get it.*) Ah, there! (*Picking it up.*) Will this do?

LUCIEN: (*Who has continued shaking YVONNE and gently repeating her name.*) I don't know. What is it?

JOSEPH: (*Bringing him the vest.*) It looks like her vest.

LUCIEN: (*The cork still between his teeth.*) It can't be helped, there's nothing else... Now, kneel down!
(*JOSEPH obeys.*)
Roll it into a wad! A wad! Don't you know what that is?

JOSEPH: Yes, sir. (*He does so.*)

LUCIEN: Good. Give it here! (*Holding out the bottle.*) Take this! This!
(*JOSEPH kneeling on the other side of YVONNE, takes the bottle and gives him the vest in exchange.*)
(*The cork still between his teeth.*) The cork! The cork!
(*JOSEPH looks around on the floor.*)
Here! Here! In my teeth!
(*JOSEPH takes the cork.*)

LUCIEN: Good. Now, the ether! The ether! (*He gives him the wad.*)
(*JOSEPH soaks the wad with ether and LUCIEN then dabs YVONNE's face with it.*)
Yvonne! Yvonne, darling! (*To JOSEPH , giving him back the wad so that he can put some ether on it.*) Oh, really you know, you... (*To YVONNE.*) Yvonne! Yvonne darling!... (*To JOSEPH .*) You might have waited till tomorrow morning before bringing this sort of news.

JOSEPH: I didn't do it for my pleasure.

LUCIEN: No, for ours perhaps?... (*To YVONNE.*) Yvonne, my sweet!... (*To JOSEPH.*) What was the hurry? Of course it's very unfortunate for my poor mother-in-law. But after all! She wouldn't have flown away by the morning. Then at least my wife would have had a peaceful night... (*A half tone lower.*) And so would I!

JOSEPH: I'm very sorry, sir. I'll know next time.

(*ANNETTE enters, running, with a salt cellar. She passes in front of JOSEPH and holds it out under LUCIEN's nose.*)

ANNETTE: Here you are, sir!

LUCIEN: (*Raising his head and looking at the salt cellar, then at ANNETTE, then back at the salt cellar again.*) What on earth's that?

ANNETTE: The salt cellar.

LUCIEN: What do you expect me to do with it?

ANNETTE: You asked for the salt.

LUCIEN: Salts, dammit, not salt! Do you think I'm going to start cooking her.

ANNETTE: How do I know? I'm not a doctor. (*She goes to the mantelpiece and puts down the salt cellar.*)

LUCIEN: (*Seeing YVONNE is coming round.*) All right!... My wife's opening her eyes. So clear off! And take that thing with, you!
(*LUCIEN quickly gives the vest back to JOSEPH, who immediately gets up and goes and stands near Annette upstage of the fireplace. During the following lines, without the audience noticing, he automatically puts the vest in his right coat pocket. LUCIEN slides under YVONNE's back and sits up against her on the floor with his legs parallel to the footlights, his feet emerging on her right and his body on her left.*)
Yvonne! Yvonne darling!

YVONNE: (*Looking to right and left as she comes round.*) What's happened?

LUCIEN: Nothing, darling. Nothing at all.

YVONNE: Then why am I on the floor? (*At this moment her look falls on JOSEPH.*) Oh... Oh! Yes... yes... oh, mother! Poor mother!
(*She bursts into tears on LUCIEN's chest.*)

LUCIEN: (*Holding her in his arms and shaking her gently as if he were soothing a baby.*) There, there!... Now, now!... Now, now! For heavens sake! Now, now... There, there!... There, there!... Now, now now!

ANNETTE: Oh, dear! Oh, dear!

LUCIEN: Be brave! There may still be hope!

YVONNE: (*Sobbing, almost with rage.*) Hope for what? She's dead!

LUCIEN: Well, that's it! That's it! The worst is over! We must accept it. Remember that for people who leave us, it's a release. Think how your poor mother suffered with her rheumatism!

YVONNE: (*Tears in her voice.*) My poor mother!

LUCIEN: (*Sadly, soothing her.*) Yes! Yes! Well, now she's not suffering any more. While we're mourning her... (*With a trace of bitterness.*) ...sitting here... she's at rest. She's happy.

YVONNE: (*Sadly, nodding.*) Who'd have thought she'd go so quickly?

LUCIEN: (*With a sigh.*) Ah, yes!... Just now when I was wondering how to pay for the curtains, I never dreamt... Ah, well!

YVONNE: (*Sobbing.*) My poor mother!

LUCIEN: Ah, yes!... Your poor, brave, good, saintly mother! (*Aside.*) I've got a touch of lumbago. (*Tired of his position, he gets onto his knees and arches his back because of the pain. Then he looks right and left to see if there's a chair within reach.*) I say, Yvonne!

YVONNE: What?

LUCIEN: You wouldn't like a chair?

YVONNE: (*Suddenly exploding, so that LUCIEN jumps.*) No, I wouldn't! A chair! A chair! What does it matter if I'm on a chair or the ground?

LUCIEN: (*Quickly.*) Yes, yes. Good, good! (*He goes and sits on the stool.*)

YVONNE: (*Lyrical in her anguish.*) I'd rather be *under* the ground.

ANNETTE: (*Near the fireplace, in distress, whispering.*) Oh, it breaks your heart!

YVONNE: (*Her body thrown back, supported on her arms with the palms of her hands on the floor, having for a few moments been twisting her mouth as if there were starch on her face.*) Mm?... (*To JOSEPH.*) Mm?... What have you put on my face, it's sticky?

LUCIEN: Nothing, darling. Ether.

YVONNE: What ether?

JOSEPH: (*Pointing to the bedside table.*) From the bottle, there!

YVONNE: How stupid! That's syrup of ether!

LUCIEN: Syrup!

JOSEPH: (*Taking the bottle from his pocket and glancing at the label.*) Oh! I didn't read the label. I just smelt it. (*He gives the bottle to Annette, who puts it on the mantelpiece.*)

LUCIEN: Oh, you're so clumsy! So clumsy!

YVONNE: (*Lyrical.*) Anyway, what does it matter! When my... (*She grimaces.*)... heart is crucified! (*Another grimace.*) Get me some water, Annette, so I can wash my face!

ANNETTE: Yes, madame.

(*ANNETTE goes upstage and out through the door, right.*)

YVONNE: (*Sadly and affectionately.*) Poor, dear woman! Do you remember how good she was?

LUCIEN: (*Absent-mindedly nods his head approvingly: then.*) Who?

YVONNE: (*Angrily slapping him on the calf.*) Mother!

LUCIEN: Oh! Yes.

YVONNE: And so kind to you! Always making excuses for you! When I think you were always attacking her... behaving as if... only two days ago you actually called her an interfering busybody!

LUCIEN: (*Sadly pleading.*) Yvonne!

YVONNE: (*Tearful.*) How could you dream of calling her an interfering busybody?

LUCIEN: (*Making a vague gesture, then as the best possible argument.*) I didn't think she'd die.

YVONNE: There! Now it's your punishment!

LUCIEN: (*Pivoting on his seat.*) Oh! God! (*During the following speech, he remains with his back to the audience, his head in his right hand, his elbow on the rail at the foot of the bed.*)

YVONNE: How dreadful to think she has passed on with the memory of your rudeness!... An interfering busybody! My saintly mother!

(*She continues in gentle, slow, rhythmical tones, while
LUCIEN at the end of each sentence nods his head as if in
approval, though in fact he is lulled to sleep by the music of
her words.*)
Well, your conscience can be at rest. I know better
than anyone what depths of forgiveness lay in my
mother's heart. I think I can interpret her dying
thoughts, when I say "Lucien, you are forgiven..."
(*Repeating sadly.*) "You are..." (*Not receiving any answer,
she raises her head and, realising he has dozed off, slaps him
hard on the calf.*) Wake up!

LUCIEN: (*Waking up with a start.*) Eh? Me? Hm... Oh! I'm
sorry. I'm rather tired.

YVONNE: (*Indignant.*) Tired! Mother's dead and he's
tired! (*She leaps up and, seizing LUCIEN, sends him flying
across the stage, straight into JOSEPH's stomach.*) Come
on, get up!

LUCIEN and JOSEPH: (*Colliding.*) Oh!

YVONNE: Shouldn't we be there?

LUCIEN: Oh! We're going...?

YVONNE: Of course we're going! You don't expect us to
sleep now?

LUCIEN: (*With a sigh of resignation, looking sadly at the
bed.*) No.

YVONNE: (*Roughly pushing LUCIEN out of her way so that
she can go to the chair, left, then picking up her petticoat and
putting it down again.*) My vest? Where's my vest? (*On
the last word she pushes JOSEPH out of the way, sending him
towards the fireplace, and goes upstage to the chair near the
bureau.*)

LUCIEN: (*To JOSEPH.*) I gave it to you.

JOSEPH: Me!

LUCIEN: Yes.

JOSEPH: Ah, yes. (*Slowly pulling the vest out of his pocket.*)
Here it is!

YVONNE: (*To JOSEPH, having come downstage between
them.*) What! You've my vest in your pocket!

JOSEPH: He used it... to put the syrup on your face.

YVONNE: (*Roughly snatching the vest.*) For heavens sake!

You must be mad! (*Turning round towards LUCIEN and seeing him motionless, waiting for heaven knows what.*) Well, hurry up! What are you waiting for? Get dressed!

LUCIEN: Oh? I have to...

YVONNE: (*Exasperated.*) Of course! You're not expecting to go there as Louis XIV?

LUCIEN: No.

YVONNE: (*To JOSEPH.*) Dressing up as Louis XIV, when you've lost your mother-in-law!

JOSEPH: (*Without thinking.*) Very funny!

YVONNE: Oh, you think so?

JOSEPH: Oh! Sorry, no!
(*ANNETTE enters.*)

LUCIEN: Ah! Annette!... Get me my black suit, black tie and black gloves!
(*ANNETTE goes towards the door, right, but immediately stops at the sound of YVONNE's voice.*)

YVONNE: (*Thoroughly exasperated, twirling LUCIEN round to face her.*) Oh, no! No! You're not going dressed like that! You'd look as though you ordered your mourning in advance. It isn't done. (*She passes across and puts her vest down on the foot of the bed.*)

LUCIEN: Quite right! (*Going to Annette, who is near the door, left.*) Well, Annette, whatever suit you like! My... my most cheerful!

ANNETTE: Yes, sir.
(*ANNETTE goes out.*)

YVONNE: (*Grumbling, as she undoes the ribbons of her night-dress, preparatory to taking it off, so that she can put her vest on.*) No, really!
(*She is facing the foot of the bed and so has her back to JOSEPH, who is looking in that direction, but absent-mindedly, taking no notice.*)

LUCIEN: (*Going to JOSEPH.*) As for you... (*Arrested by JOSEPH's attitude, he looks in the same direction, then immediately rushes to YVONNE and pulls her nightdress back round her neck from her naked shoulder.*) What are you doing? You're out of your mind!

YVONNE: (*Dumbfounded by this apparent meteor which has fallen on her shoulder.*) What?

LUCIEN: You're taking off your nightdress here?

YVONNE: (*Her nerves on edge.*) Oh! Now listen... (*She throws back the collar of her nightdress and is about to get her arm out.*)

LUCIEN: (*Pulling her nightdress back again.*) No, I won't! You're not going to appear completely naked in front of the servant!

JOSEPH: (*Completely indifferent.*) Oh, if it's because of me...

LUCIEN: (*Furiously, straight into his face.*) Of course it's because of you!

YVONNE: (*To JOSEPH, with LUCIEN between them.*) I lose my mother and all he thinks about is whether or not I'm wearing a nightdress! (*She moves towards the bed.*)

LUCIEN: (*Furious.*) You can lose your mother and still be decent!

YVONNE: Oh, yes! Oh! Shut up!

(*ANNETTE enters, left, with LUCIEN's suit on her arm and shoes in her right hand, his bowler hat standing up on their toes. His braces are hanging down from the back trouser buttons.*)

YVONNE: Come along, Annette! Come and help me!

(*YVONNE goes out, right, carrying her dressing gown and vest. ANNETTE puts LUCIEN's suit down on the chair, left, his shoes on the floor, and his hat on one of the candles in the candelabra on the mantelpiece.*)

LUCIEN: Oh! What a night! What a night!

JOSEPH: Lucky it doesn't happen every day, sir.

LUCIEN: If you think all this is funny... (*To Annette.*) Now listen, my girl! I don't know what you're up to, but you always seem to be in here.

ANNETTE: (*Whimpering, as she goes out.*) I'm only doing my job, sir.

LUCIEN: Run along then, run along! Oh!

(*ANNETTE goes out.*)

(*To JOSEPH, putting his right hand on his right shoulder.*) Now, my dear fellow, you can help me.

JOSEPH: Yes, sir.

LUCIEN: You're intelligent?

JOSEPH: Yes, sir.

LUCIEN: Good! So... er... you're going... er...

(JOSEPH goes upstage.)

LUCIEN: Where are you going? Where are you going?

JOSEPH: *(Dumbfounded.)* I don't know, sir.

LUCIEN: You're so clumsy! Now you've made me forget what I was going to say. *(Suddenly.)* Ah, yes! *(He goes upstage towards the bureau.)*

(JOSEPH eagerly goes with LUCIEN, without knowing why.)

What is it? I'm going to write a note. I don't need you.

JOSEPH: Oh! Sorry!

LUCIEN: Yes. All right! *(He takes the chair which is upstage and puts it in front of the bureau. Then he sits down and begins to write.)*

(A pause.)

JOSEPH: *(Going upstage to the left of the bureau near LUCIEN.)* You know, sir, I didn't much enjoy coming here... It's the first time I've had the honour of meeting you and your wife, sir. I'd much rather have told you you'd won first prize in the National Lottery than this sort of news.

(LUCIEN, without stopping writing, signals to him with his left hand to keep quiet.)

(Taking no notice.) So it was a big weight off my mind, when I'd finished. I must say I wouldn't like to have to start again.

LUCIEN: *(Still writing.)* You're stopping me writing, my dear fellow.

JOSEPH: Sorry! *(Hands behind his back, his hat in his hands, he comes downstage near the foot of the bed.)*

LUCIEN: Annette! *(He licks the edge of one of the letter cards which he has just written.)* Annette!

(JOSEPH looks towards him, then obligingly goes to the doorway through which the two women went out and pulls the curtain fully back.)

JOSEPH: Annette, you're wanted!

ANNETTE: (*Off.*) I'm dressing Madame, sir.

YVONNE: (*Off.*) You can wait a moment!

LUCIEN: (*Licking the second letter card.*) Yes. Yes.

JOSEPH: (*Still holding back the curtain, with his eyes glued to what is going on in the next room.*) It won't be long, sir. She's got her vest on.

LUCIEN: (*Banging the bureau with his fist, then rushing to JOSEPH and sending him whirling to the centre of the stage.*) This is too much! Why do you have to stick your nose in there?

JOSEPH: (*Dumbfounded by this method of recognising his kindness.*) I was trying to help you, sir.

LUCIEN: Help me! Help me! In that case, give me my clothes!

(*JOSEPH turns, bewildered, to right and left.*)

LUCIEN: My clothes! There! There! (*Pushing JOSEPH away to his left.*) Get out of the way! (*He goes and gets his suit himself. As he turns round, he bumps into JOSEPH who has hurried to help him.*) Get out of the way! (*He pushes him off to the right near the fireplace and reaches the end of the bed. To JOSEPH, who is completely bewildered.*) Right! Come here!

JOSEPH: (*Running.*) Yes, sir.

LUCIEN: And help me!

JOSEPH: Yes, sir.

(*During the following lines, JOSEPH takes off LUCIEN's mantle, then unhooks his jerkin. Underneath LUCIEN is wearing his ordinary shirt with a turndown collar and tie. They are near the stool at the foot of the bed.*)

LUCIEN: (*Letting himself be undressed.*) Tell me! You've a cab outside?

JOSEPH: Yes, sir.

LUCIEN: Then there's no time to lose.

JOSEPH: Especially as it's a motor. (*Having finished unhooking LUCIEN, he reaches the left.*)

LUCIEN: (*Arriving upstage of the bed.*) Oh! What a pity! It can't be helped! Still, let's enjoy ourselves while we can!

JOSEPH: (*Scandalized.*) Enjoy ourselves!

LUCIEN: Eh?... Hm! No! Well... you know what I mean...
(*He has picked up his trousers and without thinking, puts them on over his knee breeches.*)
(*ANNETTE enters, right, and, passing in front of LUCIEN, who is getting dressed with his back to the audience, stops immediately to his left.*)

ANNETTE: You wanted me, sir?

LUCIEN: (*Getting dressed.*) My wife's ready?

ANNETTE: Nearly, sir.

LUCIEN: What were you asking?

ANNETTE: If you wanted me?

LUCIEN: No.
(*ANNETTE goes towards the door.*)
Yes.
(*ANNETTE stops.*)
(*Getting dressed and splitting up his words like a man doing two things at the same time.*) Listen, there are two... two letters on the...
(*JOSEPH goes towards the bureau, to try to be useful.*)
(*To JOSEPH.*) No, not you. (*To ANNETTE.*) You, you fool! Don't you understand? On the flap of the bureau! Now go downstairs and post them!

ANNETTE: (*With a start, rebelling.*) Now!

LUCIEN: Naturally, now! They must be delivered first thing in the morning.

ANNETTE: (*Grumbling.*) This is fun! (*She goes towards the door, left.*)

LUCIEN: (*Putting on his coat and waistcoat, without noticing that his braces are hanging from his back trouser buttons.*) Where are you going? Where are you going?

ANNETTE: To put a skirt on.

LUCIEN: A skirt! Who do you think's going to take any notice of you? At five in the morning!

ANNETTE: I can't go like this in a petticoat. It's not correct.

LUCIEN: Well, put on a raincoat!

ANNETTE: I haven't got one.

LUCIEN: Then take my overcoat, it's hanging in the hall!

ANNETTE: Oh! Even so, it's not correct.

LUCIEN: Yes, yes, it's all right, run along!

ANNETTE: What will I look like? A doubtful woman!

LUCIEN: If you get kidnapped, come and tell me!

ANNETTE: Like a tart!

(*ANNETTE goes out, into the hall.*)

LUCIEN: (*Fully dressed, with his braces hanging down behind. To JOSEPH.*) There! Get me my... my...

(*JOSEPH does not understand and, after turning to right and left, finally gazes upwards.*)

... my shoes! They're not on the ceiling! (*Picking up the shoes himself and going and sitting on the stool to put them on.*) Oh! You're not very bright, are you?

JOSEPH: You didn't explain properly, sir.

LUCIEN: All right. Come here!

(*JOSEPH rushes forward and falls on his knees in front of LUCIEN, to help him. He picks up the shoe which LUCIEN has not yet put on. LUCIEN snatches it from him.*)

Get out of my way! (*Putting his shoes on.*) What make is your taxi?

JOSEPH: A Renault.

LUCIEN: A little red one? Ah! Good! They're quickest and cheapest.

JOSEPH: At this hour I was lucky to find one.

LUCIEN: Yes, that was lucky. No doubt about it, we're in luck!

(*YVONNE enters, right, with a big cloak over her dressing gown and her head wrapped in a muslin scarf.*)

YVONNE: Well! Are you ready?

LUCIEN: (*Finishing putting on his shoes.*) Yes, yes. Just a moment!

YVONNE: (*To JOSEPH, who is near the bureau.*) You've a cab?

JOSEPH: Yes, outside.

LUCIEN: (*Going to the mantelpiece for his hat.*) A Renault. A little, red one. They're quickest and cheapest. (*Putting on his hat, without noticing he's still wearing his wig, and joining YVONNE upstage.*) There! I'm ready!

YVONNE: (*Twirling him round and sending him back down-stage.*) Your wig! You're not going out with a wig on!

LUCIEN: Eh? My wig?... You're muddling me up, what do you expect? You're muddling me up! (*He takes off his wig and puts it down on the mantelpiece.*)

YVONNE: Oh! Now we're going, I feel frightened.

LUCIEN: (*Going upstage towards the hall door.*) I know. It isn't amusing for me either. But some duties in life are hard to bear. (*He passes between them and goes out into the hall.*)

(*YVONNE takes JOSEPH by the forearm and brings him downstage. LUCIEN stops in the hall at the sound of her voice and comes back following them.*)

YVONNE: Tell me...

JOSEPH: Yes?

YVONNE: She hasn't changed too much?

JOSEPH: Oh, no, not at all.

YVONNE: Poor mother! Tell me, she didn't suffer? (*LUCIEN, seeing this is going to last a long time, sits on the chair next to the fireplace.*)

JOSEPH: (*Happy to give her this consolation.*) Not for a moment. She was in good health... She had a fine appetite at dinner. Two slices of lamb...

YVONNE: (*With emotion, her eyes on the ceiling.*) Two slices of lamb!

LUCIEN: (*Irritated.*) Two slices of lamb!

JOSEPH: (*With a sigh.*) Two slices of lamb, yes. (*Continuing his story.*) After dinner she played two or three games of patience. Then she went to bed... with Monsieur.

YVONNE: (*Overcome by her sorrow, her voice scarcely audible.*) Poor mo...!

(*At this moment JOSEPH's last words strike her. She slowly raises her head, apparently thinking, then turns towards him.*)

Monsieur?

LUCIEN: (*At the same time.*) Monsieur?

YVONNE: Mother went to bed with a man?

LUCIEN: What man?

JOSEPH: (*A trace of anxiety in his voice.*) Monsieur Fajolet...
Madame's father.

YVONNE: My father!
(*LUCIEN rises and, with teeth clenched and chin thrust
forward, advances on JOSEPH, twirling him round to face
him with a sharp blow on the arm.*)

LUCIEN: Which father? What father? My mother-in-
law's a widow!

JOSEPH: (*Pivoting round and, with his back to the audience,
falling back towards the footlights.*) You mean you're not
the Pinnevinnettes?

YVONNE: Pinnevinnettes?

LUCIEN: (*Furious, advancing on him like a wild beast about to
spring on its prey.*) No, we are not the Pinnevinnettes!
(*JOSEPH has fallen back, as LUCIEN and YVONNE
advanced on him and gradually finishes by being pinned
against the bedside table. YVONNE has followed LUCIEN
in a scissors movement, which puts her on his right.*)

YVONNE: Do we look like Pinnevinnettes?

LUCIEN: The Pinnevinnettes are on the right landing.

JOSEPH: (*A lump in his throat.*) This isn't the right landing?

LUCIEN: No, it's the left! It's the right coming out of the
lift, but the left if you use the stairs.

YVONNE: You should have used the stairs like everyone
else!

JOSEPH: (*Suddenly.*) Oh no!

LUCIEN *and* YVONNE: What?

JOSEPH: In that case... I'll have to break the news again?

LUCIEN: (*Taking him by the arm and sending him midstage.*)
You don't think I'm going to do it for you?

JOSEPH: Oh! All over again! I was so glad I'd finished!

LUCIEN: I've never seen such a fool!

YVONNE: (*Also advancing on him.*) Coming here and
upsetting me with the news my mother's dead, when
she isn't!

JOSEPH: I'm very sorry.

YVONNE: (*Shrugging her shoulders.*) Oh! Shut up! (*She
comes back downstage right.*)

LUCIEN: (*Twirling him round and sending him back upstage.*) Get out of here! Idiot!

YVONNE: (*Downstage at the foot of the bed.*) Clumsy fool!

LUCIEN: (*Downstage near the fireplace.*) Moron!

JOSEPH: (*Upstage.*) It's not my fault!... You should be happy!

LUCIEN *and* YVONNE: (*Leaping in the air.*) Happy!

LUCIEN: Brute!

YVONNE: Ass!

LUCIEN: Imbecile!

JOSEPH: (*In the doorway.*) This is too much! You're cursing me because your mother's not dead. I can't help that.

LUCIEN *and* YVONNE: What did you say?

LUCIEN: (*Left of the door.*) Will you get out of here!

YVONNE: (*Pushing JOSEPH out.*) Go away!

JOSEPH: (*As he is being evicted.*) Oh! I'll never forget you!

YVONNE: Nor will I!

(*JOSEPH goes out. YVONNE follows him into the hall.*)

LUCIEN: (*Remaining in the doorway.*) Silly bastard!... Bastard!... Bastard!... Bastard!... Bastard!

(*There must be a two second interval between each exclamation, during which YVONNE, who cannot be seen, utters an indignant "Oh". This is mixed with JOSEPH's protests and the noise of the front door opening and slamming shut.*)

(*Coming downstage and, with a final snarl, not addressed to anybody.*) Bastard!

(*YVONNE, very upset, re-enters and comes downstage to the foot of the bed, throwing her cloak and scarf onto it.*)

YVONNE: Oh!

LUCIEN: Oh!

YVONNE: Oh!

LUCIEN: Oh! The fool! The fool!

YVONNE: Upsetting us like that! (*Very upset, she sits on the stool.*)

LUCIEN: (*Indignant.*) Oh!

(*A pause.*)

(*Happy at this opportunity for reprisals.*) Well! There's your mother for you! That's what she does to us! Your mother!

YVONNE: (*Dumbfounded.*) What's the matter? What's come over you?

LUCIEN: What am I going to tell the curtain man now? When he hears your mother's not dead and the whole thing's nonsense?

YVONNE: When he hears? He doesn't have to hear.

LUCIEN: (*Almost shouting.*) I've written to him!

YVONNE: (*Drawing herself up indignantly.*) Already?

LUCIEN: (*As before.*) Of course! He was threatening us.

YVONNE: Oh!

LUCIEN: I told him I'd be able to pay, as I'd had the... misfortune to lose my mother-in-law.

YVONNE: This is too much! You were discounting mother!

LUCIEN: I couldn't guess it was all nonsense. (*Shaking his fist at the hall door.*) Oh, the interfering busybody! Interfering busybody!

YVONNE: (*Jumping on him like a tigress.*) Are you calling mother an interfering busybody again? Are you calling mother an interfering busybody?

LUCIEN: Oh! Yes, then! Oh yes, then! Interfering busybody! Interfering busybody!

YVONNE: (*At his face with her nails.*) I hate you! I hate you!

(*A door slams in the distance, cutting short their argument.*)

YVONNE: (*Roughly, peremptorily.*) Sh! Shut up!

LUCIEN: (*Gripped by her.*) What is it?

YVONNE: The maid's just come in at the back door.

LUCIEN: (*Coming downstage.*) I don't give a damn!

YVONNE: (*Jumping with joy.*) The *neighbours* have lost their mother! The *neighbours* have lost their mother!

LUCIEN: There you go, delighted at other people's misfortunes!

YVONNE: (*Happily coming downstage right and sitting on the bed with a jump.*) When I think it was nearly me!

LUCIEN: Yes... no such luck! (*Going upstage.*) Oh, we're in
a mess! A mess!

(*ANNETTE enters, wearing a big, long overcoat of
LUCIEN's.*)

ANNETTE: There! It's done!

LUCIEN: (*Leaping at her and seizing her wrists.*) Oh!... The
letters! What have you done with the letters?

ANNETTE: (*Drawing back in the space between the back wall
and the bed.*) I've posted them.

LUCIEN: There! She's posted them!

ANNETTE: Oh yes. As you...

LUCIEN: A fine job you've done! Why did you have to
hurry like that?

ANNETTE: You told me...

LUCIEN: Yes, I did... I did... because my wife's mother
was dead! (*He comes downstage.*)

YVONNE: (*Radiant, to ANNETTE, who is near her on the
other side of the bed.*) Yes, and now... she isn't.

ANNETTE: (*Upstage of the bed.*) Oh dear, oh dear!...
They're mad!

YVONNE: (*Very warmly.*) It isn't mother! It's the neighbours' mother. The man got the wrong flat.

ANNETTE: No! Is that true?

LUCIEN: (*Furious.*) Yes, it is!

ANNETTE: (*Jumping with joy.*) Oh, I'm so happy!

LUCIEN: (*As before.*) She's happy! She's happy!

ANNETTE: Yes, I am!

YVONNE: (*Pointing to LUCIEN who is downstage left.*) Yes,
but he's sorry!

LUCIEN: (*Shrugging his shoulders.*) Now, really!

YVONNE: He'd have been happy to bury mother!

LUCIEN: (*As before.*) Oh, bury her... (*Suddenly.*) Oh, no!

YVONNE: What?

LUCIEN: My letter to Borniol!

YVONNE: What letter to Borniol?

LUCIEN: (*Quickly, upset.*) I wrote to Borniol to come to
your mother's in the morning for the funeral
arrangements.

YVONNE: (*Jumping onto the bed on her knees.*) You didn't!

LUCIEN: I did! Oh, what a mess!

YVONNE: (*Advancing on her knees to the foot of the bed.*) So you want to kill her! You want to kill her!

LUCIEN: It doesn't matter. I'll send a telegram in the morning.

YVONNE: (*Shaking her fist at him.*) You brute! You want to kill mother! You want to kill mother!

(*The rest is said almost together.*)

LUCIEN: (*Going to the foot of the bed. Peremptorily.*) That's enough! It's time for bed!

YVONNE: (*Not listening.*) Traitor! Murderer! Jack the Ripper!

LUCIEN: (*One foot on the stool.*) Will you shut up! Will you shut up!

ANNETTE: (*Having climbed onto the edge of the bed, trying to get between them.*) Please! Please!

YVONNE: He wants to kill mother! He wants to kill mother!

LUCIEN: (*Abandoning his position and facing the audience.*) Oh, no! No! I'd rather sleep in the maid's sheets!

YVONNE: (*As the curtain begins to fall.*) And he says I've breasts like coathooks!

ANNETTE: Oh dear! Oh dear!

LUCIEN: (*Reaching the door, left.*) Oh, shut up! Shut up!

YVONNE: He says I've breasts like coathooks!

LUCIEN: Shut up!

(*LUCIEN goes out.*)

Curtain

ONE MONTH EARLY

Léonie est en avance

Characters

LEONIE

TOUDOUX, her husband

CLEMENCE, their maid

MME DE CHAMPRINET, Léonie's mother

DE CHAMPRINET, Léonie's father

MME VIRTUEL, a midwife

*T*he *TOUDOUXs' dining room in Paris. About 1910. Midstage towards the rear, a round dining table, laid for two. Downstage left, almost at the footlights, a card table with an abandoned game of cards on it and a chair at each side. Downstage left, the door to LEONIE's bedroom. Upstage right, a double door into the hall. Midstage right, a lower single door into the pantry. Downstage right, a console table. Upstage left, against the wall, a sideboard, with a chair each side of it. In the right corner, between the hall door and the pantry door, a small dresser. Midstage right, a yard from the console table, a small armchair facing the audience. A light, which is switched on, over the dining table.*

When the curtain rises, LEONIE, in a kimono, and TOUDOUX are walking to and fro across the stage. He supports her with his left arm round her waist, at the same time holding each of her hands in his. They are approximately midstage and go to the extreme left, where they wheel and continue their walk to the extreme right. They wheel again and go back to the left, where LEONIE, bent double, stops to breathe.

LEONIE: Whew!

TOUDOUX: (*Hesitant and timid.*) You... you don't feel better?

LEONIE: Shut up. Don't ask questions. You tire me out.

TOUDOUX: (*Submissively.*) Yes.

LEONIE: (*In pain.*) Hold my. hands. Hold me tight. Hurt me.

TOUDOUX: (*Obeying.*) Yes.

LEONIE: Harder than that. I can't feel a thing.

TOUDOUX: Yes. (*Stifling a sigh.*) Whew!

LEONIE: (*Her body bent double, looking at him and shaking her head, exhausted.*) Oh! You don't know what it's like!

TOUDOUX: No.

LEONIE: Wait. I want to sit down. I'm tired.

TOUDOUX: (*Putting her into the chair at the right of the card table.*) That's it... There... (*He leaves her and goes upstage to the table, where his half eaten dinner is waiting for him.*)
(*LEONIE, collapsed in the chair, her eyes cast down, stretches out her hands to the left towards her husband, thinking he is still nearby. Not finding him, she turns round and sees him sitting quietly at the table in front of his plate.*)

LEONIE: Oh, no! No! Hold my hands, don't abandon me. You can finish your dinner later.

TOUDOUX: (*Submitting.*) Oh?... Yes... Yes... (*He rises and goes to her.*)

LEONIE: Hold my hands tight. There. Harder... Harder.

TOUDOUX: Yes.

(*They remain there, face to face, saying nothing: TOUDOUX, upright, holding her hands; LEONIE, exhausted and plaintive. He looks towards the table where the rest of his dinner is waiting for him and then gazes at the ceiling, his mind elsewhere.*)

LEONIE: (*Almost shocked.*) You don't seem to be enjoying yourself.

TOUDOUX: Well...

LEONIE: (*Without removing her hands from his, but nevertheless making all the gestures her words require.*) Wonderful! You're not enjoying yourself! Do you think I am?

TOUDOUX: (*Whose arms have executed all the movements imposed by his wife's gestures.*) I didn't say that.

LEONIE: I'm suffering and you set yourself up as the victim.

TOUDOUX: I haven't complained. You ask me if I'm enjoying myself, you don't want me to say I am, when I see you suffering.

LEONIE: Suffering. Yes, you can say that. Because of you.

TOUDOUX: (*Nodding his head approvingly with a penitent air, but nevertheless showing a little pride.*) Because of me, yes.

(*A pause. LEONIE's pains appear to diminish.*)

Well? Are you feeling better?

LEONIE: A little, yes.

TOUDOUX: (*Satisfied.*) Ah!

(*CLEMENCE enters with a dish of food.*)

CLEMENCE: You're not eating, sir?

TOUDOUX: Yes, yes, in a moment. Don't bother.

LEONIE: (*Doubled up, plaintively.*) Tell me Clémence...

CLEMENCE: (*Upstage.*) Yes?

LEONIE: Have you told mother?

CLEMENCE: I telephoned, yes.

LEONIE: And the midwife?

CLEMENCE: I sent the concierge. To the doctor too.

LEONIE: Good!... (*To TOUDOUX, seeing him looking like a dumb victim.*) Oh, all right, have your dinner. Go on. You look as though you're being sacrificed.
(*CLEMENCE goes out into the pantry.*)

TOUDOUX: Me?... No, I don't.

LEONIE: Yes, you do. I'm not surprised. You're not *suffering.* You can think about *eating*... Go on, then. There's a moment's pause, take advantage of it. Go and eat, go on.

TOUDOUX: No, I wouldn't like to...

LEONIE: (*Pushing him away with her hand.*) Go on, I tell you.

TOUDOUX: (*As if in self defence, going upstage towards the dining table.*) Only because you insist.

LEONIE: Yes, yes.

TOUDOUX: (*Sitting in front of the place laid for him at the right of the table and spreading a napkin on his knees.*) If you need me, don't worry, I'm here.

LEONIE: Yes, I can see you, thanks.
(*CLEMENCE enters.*)

TOUDOUX: Won't you eat a little something? It would do you good.

LEONIE: Oh! Me, eat! No, no! (*Emphasising 'suffering' to give it the importance of an action.*) I am suffering. To each his part.

TOUDOUX: (*Resigned.*) All right. (*To CLEMENCE.*) What have you got there?

CLEMENCE: Macaroni.

LEONIE: (*Rising painfully and, supporting herself with her hands on the table, as she reaches the chair on the other side.*) For me, Calvary! For you, the joys of life!

TOUDOUX: (*Helping himself to the macaroni.*) Joys of life! Macaroni!

LEONIE: (*Seated, holding the playing cards.*) No. *I*, between two bouts of pain, *I* will play patience. There!

TOUDOUX: You're so brave.

LEONIE: (*Proudly.*) Later, you can tell Baby. (*Tenderly to the audience.*) Baby!

TOUDOUX: Heavens, it's strong!

LEONIE: (*Turning towards him, in the same tender voice.*) Baby?

TOUDOUX: No, the macaroni.

LEONIE: (*Scornfully.*) Oh!

TOUDOUX: (*To CLEMENCE.*) What on earth is this cheese? Oh!

CLEMENCE: Parmesan and gruyère mixed. I got it at the grocer's.

TOUDOUX: I see. It is aggressive.
(*CLEMENCE goes out into the pantry.*)
And full of pepper!

LEONIE: (*Pityingly.*) How materialistic you are! The day you're going to be a father!

TOUDOUX: No, I said that because...

LEONIE: Oh, I hope he arrives safely.

TOUDOUX: (*Absent-mindedly nodding approvingly; then.*) Who?

LEONIE: Who? Baby, of course! *I* don't think about macaroni all the time!

TOUDOUX: (*Eating.*) Why shouldn't he arrive safely?

LEONIE: Because! Because he's a lot earlier than we expected.

TOUDOUX: Yes... Yes, he is. That means he's ready.

LEONIE: Oh, yes! You explain everything to suit yourself! (*Rising.*) Remember... (*Painfully reaching the chair opposite him at the dining table and sitting.*)... he wasn't expected before the twentieth of next month. (*Distressed.*) One month and four days early!

TOUDOUX: Yes... Yes. Well... he's in rather a hurry. (*Changing his tone.*) After all, what's wrong with that?

LEONIE: (*With a vague gesture.*) Oh...

TOUDOUX: He'll always be one month and four days older than other people of his age. What an advantage!

LEONIE: Yes, but he has to be born first. At eight months!

TOUDOUX: That's nothing to worry about. Look... Thingummy. Oh! You know... mm... Philippe le Bel!

LEONIE: I don't know any Lebel's.

TOUDOUX: No. Philippe... Le... Bel! I read somewhere that he was born at eight months.

LEONIE: (*Distressed.*) Oh!... And... he's alive?

TOUDOUX: No, he's dead.

LEONIE: (*Upset already.*) Oh! You see!

TOUDOUX: (*Quickly.*) He did live... very successfully too! For forty-six years!... So you see!

LEONIE: I don't care, I wish it were over.

TOUDOUX: So do I. Oh! This macaroni's lying on my stomach like a sponge. (*He takes the water jug.*)

LEONIE: Oh!... Oh!... It's starting again.

TOUDOUX: (*Pouring out a glass of water.*) Good, good! (*LEONIE rises and goes towards the right, collecting TOUDOUX on the way, seizing his left hand with her left hand.*)

LEONIE: Come along. Let's walk.

TOUDOUX: (*Having put down the jug, wanting to take the glass.*) Wait, while I have a drink.

LEONIE: (*Pulling him towards her.*) Come along. You can have a drink later.

TOUDOUX: (*Complying.*) Yes, yes. (*They go upstage beyond the table. As he passes, TOUDOUX wants to take his glass.*)

LEONIE: (*Dragging him along.*) No, no!... Hold my hands. Hold my hands.

TOUDOUX: (*Obeying.*) Yes.

LEONIE: (*Taking off again.*) Let's walk. Let's walk.

TOUDOUX: Yes. Yes. (*They come downstage by the left of the table, reach the extreme right, turn round and come back to the left as far as the card table.*)

LEONIE: (*Stopping because of the pain.*) Oh! It's dreadful... dreadful!

TOUDOUX: Yes. Be brave. Be brave.

LEONIE: (*Crossly.*) Oh! Be brave!

TOUDOUX: It won't be anything.

LEONIE: (*Leaping up.*) I certainly hope it will be.

TOUDOUX: (*Dumbfounded.*) What?... Ah! Yes, of course it will be.

LEONIE: If I have to suffer like this for nothing...!

TOUDOUX: (*Very affectionately, straight into her face.*) Yes. Of course. (*He draws out the last word.*)

LEONIE: (*Throwing her head back, as she pushes him away without releasing his hands.*) Oh! Phew! How awful!

TOUDOUX: What?

LEONIE: You smell of cheese.

TOUDOUX: Oh! It's the macaroni.

LEONIE: I don't care what it is. You smell of cheese!

TOUDOUX: I am sorry.

LEONIE: Really, you see I'm ill and you don't even bother not to eat macaroni.

TOUDOUX: I wish you'd let me have a drink. I'm choking. (*Sighing.*) Ohh!

LEONIE: Oh! Please! You stink!

TOUDOUX: Sorry.

LEONIE: Try to walk with your head turned the other way.

TOUDOUX: (*Submissive.*) Yes.

(*They walk in silence, TOUDOUX with his head turned away. They cross the stage once or twice.*)

Walking like this makes me giddy.

LEONIE: That doesn't matter. Hold me. Hurt me.

TOUDOUX: Yes.

LEONIE: (*Stopping with one hand on her hip, bent double.*) Oh! It's agony.

TOUDOUX: (*Hiccuping.*) Hic!

LEONIE: (*Standing upright, getting furious.*) What do you mean, Hic? Oh! Say it again. I dare you to.

TOUDOUX: I didn't say Hic. I've... hic... hiccups.

LEONIE: You've hiccups! A fine time to choose! (*Quietly.*) Oh! I'm so ill.

TOUDOUX: It's not my fault. It's the maca... hic... roni.

LEONIE: Then don't breathe, that's not difficult. It will
go away.

TOUDOUX: 'Don't breathe, that's not difficult'! Hic! It's
easy to say that... hic... oh, yes!

LEONIE: You're so selfish.

TOUDOUX: Hic! Me?

LEONIE: You only think about yourself.

TOUDOUX: For heavens sake! Hic! What am I... hic...
doing?

LEONIE: Oh! Once again please don't talk into my face
the whole time with all that cheese.

TOUDOUX: Sorry. (*He turns his head away and in the same
movement a hiccup brings it back towards her.*) Hic!

LEONIE: Your hiccups are driving me mad.

TOUDOUX: I can't help having hiccups.

LEONIE: Have them then, but don't go hic at me all the
time.

TOUDOUX: I don't do it... hic... on purpose. I can't not
go hic, when I've... hic... hiccups.

LEONIE: Have a drink then, if you've hiccups. Have
a drink.

TOUDOUX: (*Leaving her and hurrying towards his glass.*)
There's nothing... hic... I'd like.... hic... better. For the
last hour I've... hic...

LEONIE: Don't talk so much. Drink up.

TOUDOUX: Hic... yes.

LEONIE: (*Sitting, left of the card table.*) Oh! What a day!
(*TOUDOUX, having finished his drink, comes downstage
towards her, above the card table. A pause.*)

TOUDOUX: Ah! It's gone... That's better... Hic... That's better.

LEONIE: (*Her forehead on her right forearm which is on the back
of her chair. Bitterly.*) You're lucky. I wish I could
say that.

TOUDOUX: (*Affectionately taking her left hand which is on the
table.*) You still feel bad?

LEONIE: (*Sitting upright, suddenly angry.*) Of course I do.

TOUDOUX: (*Tapping her hand in a friendly way.*) Poor
darling! I do feel sorry for you.

LEONIE: (*Acidly.*) Well you may!

TOUDOUX: I wish I could do it for you.

LEONIE: 'Wish I could do it for you'! What does that mean? You're not committing yourself to much.

TOUDOUX: I do what I can.

LEONIE: (*Once more overcome by the pain.*) Oh! Oh! Let's walk. Let's walk. (*She pulls him towards her.*)

TOUDOUX: (*Complying, stepping over the chair at the right of the table to avoid keeping her waiting.*) Yes... Yes.
(*They reach the right of the stage. As they are turning round to come back, LEONIE stops.*)

LEONIE: No. Let's sit down.

TOUDOUX: (*Finding himself in front of the armchair, sitting down at the same time as LEONIE.*) Good.

LEONIE: (*Rising from the arm of the chair which was all she found to sit on.*) Not you! Me!

TOUDOUX: (*Rising quickly to give her his seat and repeating her words in complete confusion.*) That's right. Not you. Me... No! Not me, you.

LEONIE: (*Sitting down.*) You can stand.

TOUDOUX: (*Extreme right.*) I can stand, yes.

LEONIE: (*Exhausted.*) Oh! What torture! I'm sweating all over.
(*A pause.*)
(*Faintly.*) Give me something to drink.

TOUDOUX: What?

LEONIE: (*Immediately annoyed.*) A drink!

TOUDOUX: A drink, yes. (*He rushes towards the dining table.*)

LEONIE: Must you keep on repeating everything I say?

TOUDOUX: I only do it when I haven't heard you properly.

LEONIE: You've always a good reason for everything!

TOUDOUX: (*Giving her the glass.*) Here.

LEONIE: Thank you. (*Putting it to her lips.*) Oh! Ugh. It's your glass.

TOUDOUX: Eh? Yes... yes.

LEONIE: It smells of cheese.

TOUDOUX: Cheese?... Oh, that's the macaroni. (*He takes the glass away.*)

LEONIE: You're so clumsy.

TOUDOUX: (*Returning with another glass and the jug.*)
What do you expect? It's never happened to
me before.

LEONIE: (*Irritated.*) Or me. But it doesn't make me behave
like that.

TOUDOUX: (*Emptying the remains of the jug into the glass
and bringing it to her.*) Look. You'll be married this year.

LEONIE: (*Grumbling.*) Oh! You're able to laugh!

TOUDOUX: It was only a joke.

LEONIE: (*Taking the glass, shrugging her shoulders.*) Joke!
(*She drinks.*)

TOUDOUX: (*Tenderly.*) There, there.

LEONIE: (*Giving him back the glass.*) Thank you.
(*TOUDOUX takes the glass and jug back to the table and
returns to LEONIE.*)

TOUDOUX: Are you feeling better?

LEONIE: (*Despondently.*) Oh!... For the moment, yes.

TOUDOUX: It's terrible.

LEONIE: Oh! You've no idea. It hits you in the middle, as
though you're being split in two.

TOUDOUX: (*Upstage of the armchair, his left arm on its back.*)
Yes, I know.

LEONIE: How do you know?

TOUDOUX: That's how I felt with my kidney trouble.

LEONIE: (*With superb disdain.*) Your kidney trouble! You
dare to compare the two! That was nothing. That was
pleasant.

TOUDOUX: Pleasant?

LEONIE: (*Furiously.*) Yes! Yes! It's extraordinary the
malicious pleasure you get in making my suffering
seem less than yours.

TOUDOUX: Me?

LEONIE: I'm in pain, that's enough. Do at least let me
enjoy my suffering to the full.

TOUDOUX: Yes, of course. I only meant...

LEONIE: Vanity. Always vanity.

TOUDOUX: Vanity!

(*CLEMENCE has by now entered from the pantry, with a piece of Roquefort on a plate. She goes towards the sideboard.*)

CLEMENCE: You've finished with the macaroni, sir?

TOUDOUX: Yes, I have. I certainly have!... What have you got there?

CLEMENCE: Cheese.

LEONIE: What! (*Very firmly.*) Oh, no!... No! We've had enough cheese.

TOUDOUX: (*Conciliating, but without conviction.*) We've... We've had enough cheese.

CLEMENCE: Oh! Such a lovely piece of Roquefort! (*she puts it down on the sideboard.*)

LEONIE: Roquefort! Thanks very much! I've already had the macaroni thrust down my throat.

TOUDOUX: Thrust down your throat!
(*CLEMENCE goes out, taking the remains of the meat and the macaroni.*)

LEONIE: But I say nothing. I never complain.

TOUDOUX: You never complain!

LEONIE: (*Getting excited.*) You think I complain?

TOUDOUX: (*To calm her.*) No. No.

LEONIE: I do all I can to make things easy for you. And you think I complain!

TOUDOUX: No. No.

LEONIE: You obviously don't know what other women are like. I'd like to see you married to a difficult woman!

TOUDOUX: You're right, I tell you. You're right. I expressed myself badly.

LEONIE: Saying I complain! (*Once more overcome by the pain.*) Oh!... Oh!... It's starting again.

TOUDOUX: There... there. You see. You're getting excited.

LEONIE: (*Taking his hands.*) Quick! Let's walk. Walk!

TOUDOUX: (*Suppressing a sigh of annoyance; then, resigned.*) Yes.

LEONIE: (*As they walk.*) Hold me. Hold me. (*Having reached the left.*) Oh! The brute!... It's so violent.

TOUDOUX: Don't think about it. Don't think about it.

LEONIE: (*With grunts of pain.*) Oh! You're marvellous! 'Don't think about it'! Easy to say! You're not in childbirth.

TOUDOUX: (*Instinctively thrusting like her.*) No.

LEONIE: (*Thrusting.*) Wait. Wait. (*Grunting.*) Erh! Erh!

TOUDOUX: (*As before.*) Hh! Yes. Hh! Yes.

LEONIE: (*Thrusting.*) Oh! I'll never forget this child.

TOUDOUX: (*As before.*) Hh! No.

LEONIE: (*Bent double, choking.*) Damn the brat! I love it already... Erh!

TOUDOUX: (*As before.*) So do I. Erh!

LEONIE: Erh!... (*Sharply.*) Let's walk.

TOUDOUX: Let's walk.

(*They walk up and down. As they turn round, having reached the right, CLEMENCE enters, running in from the hall.*)

CLEMENCE: Madame, Madame's here, Madame's mother!

LEONIE: (*Without interrupting her walk.*) Ah! Good. Good.

(*MME DE CHAMPRINET enters quickly and comes up against their backs as they reach the extreme left.*)

MME DE C: Well, darling! What's this I hear? Today's the day?

(*They both stop, without turning round, at right angles to the footlights, TOUDOUX upstage.*)

TOUDOUX: Good evening, mother.

MME DE C: (*Already annoyed by him.*) Yes. Good evening. Good evening. Oh!

(*CLEMENCE goes out.*)

LEONIE: (*Bent double, not having the courage to turn round to her mother.*) Oh, mother! It's terrible.

MME DE C: My poor darling!

LEONIE: (*Stretching out her left hand behind her towards her mother.*) Hold my hands, mother. Hold my hands.

MME DE C: (*Tenderly.*) Yes. (*Suddenly to TOUDOUX, pushing him out of her way to take his place.*) Get out of the way.

TOUDOUX: Sorry.

MME DE C: (*To LEONIE.*) There, there, my sweet.

TOUDOUX: (*Reaching the right and sitting in the armchair.*) I'm not sorry to sit down for a moment.

LEONIE: Let's walk. Let's walk.

MME DE C: Yes. Yes.

(*They start walking and reach the right, near the armchair. LEONIE stops and looks at her mother, shaking her head.*)

LEONIE: Oh, mother! If you only knew...!

MME DE C: (*With an affectionate smile.*) I do, my child. I do.

LEONIE: Of course. You've been through this too.

MME DE C: Yes, darling. You gave me some happy moments. One difficult one! But afterwards it's so wonderful, you forget. An exquisite agony!

LEONIE: Never mind, you can't have suffered as much as me.

MME DE C: Just as much, darling.

LEONIE: No, you couldn't. In those days!

MME DE C: In those days it was the same as today. Progress hasn't changed anything.

LEONIE: All the same, if you could compare... (*Her face changes.*) Wait... wait. It's going away.

MME DE C: Ah! You see.

LEONIE: (*Discouraged.*) It will start again. (*Changing her tone.*) I want to sit down.

MME DE C: (*Next to the armchair level with TOUDOUX's knees, passing LEONIE across to make her sit in it.*) Yes. Yes. (*Finding TOUDOUX as she does so.*) Get out of there.

TOUDOUX: (*Rising quickly and moving away to the extreme right.*) Sorry.

MME DE C: (*Still holding LEONIE.*) You can see your wife's ill and wants to sit down, yet you sit there like an overfed bull.

TOUDOUX: Bull?

MME DE C: Yes, bull. (*To LEONIE.*) Sit down, darling.

TOUDOUX: I've never seen a bull in an armchair.

MME DE C: This is no time for jokes. Are you pleased with your handiwork?

TOUDOUX: (*Sincerely.*) I'll be pleased when it's over. I'm not enjoying myself much now.

MME DE C: Really! Do you think my daughter is? You may not be enjoying yourself, but there's a sly, satisfied look on your face...

TOUDOUX: Me?

LEONIE: (*Seated, bent double, without thinking of the meaning of her words.*) Don't scold him, mother. It's nothing to do with him.

MME DE C: (*Surprised.*) Oh?

TOUDOUX: Nothing to do with me?

LEONIE: Eh?... No, I mean he didn't do it on purpose.

TOUDOUX: (*Reassured.*) Ah! Good.

LEONIE: It's happened because it had to happen. Inevitably, some day or other...

MME DE C: Another would have been better. You do everything so quickly. It's most unseemly. What will people say? Simple good breeding...

TOUDOUX: I'm sorry I didn't consult you, mother.

MME DE C: (*Having taken off her coat and put it on the chair at the left of the dining table, coming downstage, bringing the chair from the right of the table.*) Witty!

TOUDOUX: No... When I got married, you said you hoped I'd soon give you a grandchild.

MME DE C: That may be. But you didn't have to put my daughter in this state.

TOUDOUX: (*Maliciously.*) There was no other way I could do it.

MME DE C: (*Seated next to LEONIE on the chair she has moved.*) My poor darling!

LEONIE: Don't feel sorry for me, mother. This is our lot.

MME DE C: You're so stoical. (*Going straight on.*) Have you told them to boil some water?

LEONIE: Yes, mother. You didn't tell father, I hope?

MME DE C: (*Without pity.*) Yes. Immediately. I sent a message to the Club.

LEONIE: Oh! Why? It would have been better to wait till it was all over. He'd have been spared the agony.

MME DE C: Why? Why shouldn't he bear his share? Like other people.

LEONIE: Oh! Poor father!

MME DE C: Poor father! Poor father! Aren't I equally important? We've always too much consideration for men, that's why they're so selfish.

TOUDOUX: (*Between his teeth.*) Thanks.

LEONIE: (*Nicely.*) Father's not a man.

MME DE C: He is for me. (*Seeing LEONIE's face contracting.*) It's starting again?

LEONIE: Yes.

MME DE C: Would you like to walk?

TOUDOUX: Yes, that's right, let's walk.

LEONIE: (*Flaring up.*) No, I don't want to walk.

TOUDOUX: All right, then, don't let's walk.

LEONIE: (*To her mother.*) This is a little one. I can stand this. (*CLEMENCE enters from the pantry and comes downstage between LEONIE and TOUDOUX, next to the armchair.*)

CLEMENCE: (*To LEONIE.*) They've brought the things from the Galeries Lafayette.

LEONIE: (*Understanding.*) Ah! Yes.

TOUDOUX: What things?

CLEMENCE: The baby's toilet things, a bath, jugs...

LEONIE: Yes, yes. For Monsieur Achille.

(*MME DE CHAMPRINET is surprised.*)

TOUDOUX: (*Knowing what she means.*) Ah!

LEONIE: (*To CLEMENCE.*) Good. Bring it all here, so I can see.

CLEMENCE: Yes. (*He goes to the door.*)

LEONIE: Is Monsieur Achille's room ready for him?

CLEMENCE: Yes.

LEONIE: Don't forget to put a hot water bottle in Monsieur Achille's cradle.

CLEMENCE: Yes

(*CLEMENCE goes out into the pantry.*)

LEONIE: Julien, go and help Clémence.

TOUDOUX: Oh!... All right. (*Calling as he goes out.*) Clémence, I'll help you with the things for Monsieur Achille.

(*TOUDOUX goes out.*)

MME DE C: Monsieur Achille! Monsieur Achille! You've decided it's a boy?

LEONIE: (*Sure of her facts.*) It's a boy, yes, mother.

MME DE C: Oh! You know in advance, do you?

LEONIE: (*Irrefutably.*) We've never considered anything else.

MME DE C: (*Accepting the position.*) Oh, in that case...! And if it's a girl... what then? You'll send it back?

LEONIE: (*Annoyed.*) It will be a boy. (*As supporting evidence.*) I was hardly sick at all at the beginning. I'm told that's a certain sign.

MME DE C: (*Pretending to be convinced.*) Ah!

LEONIE: And the quarters of the moon! When the moon, during pregnancy...

MME DE C: Oh, no! No! If you're going to give me astronomy lessons, no! I'd rather take your word for it. (*Taking her chair back to its place.*) I'll accept Monsieur Achille. Till further notice. (*She reaches the left.*) (*TOUDOUX enters, followed by CLEMENCE, carrying the bath in which are heaped the baby's toilet things, including jugs and chamber pot.*)

TOUDOUX: Here's his equipment.

LEONIE: (*Rising and painfully crossing the stage to sit in the chair at the right of the card table.*) Show me. Oh! It hurts.

MME DE C: (*Kindly, as she helps her to sit down.*) Don't take any notice of it.

LEONIE: (*To CLEMENCE.*) That's the bath, good! (*To TOUDOUX.*) His little washing things!... His jugs!... Here in this room!
(*As CLEMENCE picks it all up, LEONIE notices the chamber pot at the bottom of the bath and takes it.*)
Oh! His pot!
(*CLEMENCE goes out, taking everything with her except the chamber.*)
(*With emotion.*) His pot! This will be his little pottie! How big it is! (*In a burst of tenderness, putting it to her lips.*) You darling thing!
(*MME DE CHAMPRINET has come downstage, without taking her eyes off LEONIE.*)

MME DE C: (*Tenderly, with emotion, to TOUDOUX, pointing to LEONIE.*) Just like me at her birth!

TOUDOUX: (*Not caring.*) Oh!

MME DE C: (*Pointing to LEONIE.*) I loved her before she was born.

TOUDOUX: Oh!

MME DE C: (*Looking fondly at LEONIE.*) Yes.

TOUDOUX: It happened to me later.

LEONIE: (*To TOUDOUX, holding out the chamber.*) Here. Put it away.

> (*LEONIE passes it to MME DE CHAMPRINET, who passes it to TOUDOUX and then goes upstage beyond the card table.*)

TOUDOUX: (*Dutifully.*) Yes. (*He looks around, not knowing where to put it.*)

LEONIE: (*Watching him carrying the chamber like any other object.*) Doesn't that fill you with emotion?

TOUDOUX: What?

LEONIE: His pottie.

TOUDOUX: (*Without conviction.*) Oh! Yes.

LEONIE: (*Proudly.*) No more than me!

TOUDOUX: Oh, yes! Darling thing!

LEONIE: Oh yes... darling!

TOUDOUX: What are you laughing at?

LEONIE: (*With a chuckle.*) Nothing.

TOUDOUX: Yes, what is it?

MME DE C: Tell us, go on.

LEONIE: No... Seeing you holding the chamber reminded me of a silly dream had last night.

TOUDOUX: You dreamt about a chamber pot?

LEONIE: (*Laughing.*) Yes.

MME DE C: (*With conviction.*) Ah! That's a good sign.

LEONIE: We were at Longchamp races. I was wearing my grey dress and you had your morning suit. But instead of a top hat, you were wearing your chamber pot.

TOUDOUX: (*Who had been listening with a smile, stiffens.*) Me?

MME DE C: What a funny idea!

TOUDOUX: (*Annoyed.*) It's ridiculous. (*He reaches the right.*)

LEONIE: You were so proud. You raised it to everybody.

I was embarrassed. I said: (*Slowly with emphasis.*) 'Julien! Julien! Take off your chamber. People are looking'. And you said: 'Never mind. It's all right. I'll start a new fashion'.

TOUDOUX: You do have extraordinary dreams.

LEONIE: Oh, mother, if you'd seen him! He was so funny.

MME DE C: I'm sure he was.

TOUDOUX: (*Looking for somewhere to put the chamber.*) Charming! Oh, charming!

LEONIE: (*Very naturally.*) Put the chamber on your head for a moment to show mother.

TOUDOUX: (*Turning round, dumbfounded.*) Me?

LEONIE: (*Not for a moment doubting he'll obey.*) You'll see, mother.

TOUDOUX: Certainly not! The idea!

LEONIE: (*Offended.*) You might put it on when I ask you to.

TOUDOUX: You don't consider me at all.

LEONIE: (*Unanswerably.*) To show mother.

TOUDOUX: I wouldn't show the Pope. You don't give a damn for me. Wanting me to put a chamber on my head! Are you out of your mind?

LEONIE: It's a new one. It's never been used.

TOUDOUX: New or old, it's still a chamber pot.

MME DE C: (*Having risen, coming downstage.*) We're all alone.

TOUDOUX: That makes no difference. My dignity...

LEONIE: (*Rising and reaching the left.*) There! He won't do anything to please me!

TOUDOUX: You're incredible!

MME DE C: I'd understand if we asked you to do it at the races or the Club. But here!

TOUDOUX: Not here or anywhere else!

LEONIE: (*Getting obstinate.*) I want you to put it on your head, there!

TOUDOUX: Do you? Well, I don't.

LEONIE: (*Tapping her foot.*) I want you to. I want you to.

TOUDOUX: No, no, no... No!

MME DE C: Julien! Julien! My daughter's asking you.

TOUDOUX: No, I tell you.

LEONIE: I want you to, there! I want you to. I've a craving. A craving!

MME DE C: (*Going to LEONIE.*) You see! She has a craving. A craving!

TOUDOUX: All right, she has a craving.

MME DE C: (*Putting her arms round LEONIE.*) Julien, please. Think of her condition. Think what a craving is.

TOUDOUX: Oh! Bosh!

LEONIE: I want you to. I've a craving.

MME DE C: You hear! Think that because of your obstinacy your son might be born with a chamber on his head.

TOUDOUX: Good. It would come in useful.

LEONIE *and* MME DE C: Oh!

TOUDOUX: We'd send this one back, it's not been used.

MME DE C: Oh! Daring to say a thing like that!

LEONIE: A wicked father! Wicked!

TOUDOUX: It's a fact.

LEONIE: (*Like a spoilt child.*) Put it on. Put it on.

TOUDOUX: (*In the same tone.*) No, I won't put it on. I won't put it on.

LEONIE: He won't put it on! Oh! Oh! Oh!... Oh! I'm in agony.

MME DE C: There! See what you've done. See the condition your wife's in.

LEONIE: (*Collapsing into the chair at the left of the card table.*) He refuses to satisfy my cravings! Oh! Oh!

MME DE C: (*With spirit.*) Put it on, we order you to.

TOUDOUX: Put it on yourself, if you think it's so important.

MME DE C: If my daughter asked me to...

LEONIE: (*Her head on her arm which is bent backwards on the back of the chair.*) Oh! He's heartless! Heartless!

MME DE C: (*Trying to be calm in spite of her feelings.*) Julien, please! I appeal to your feelings as a husband. As a father!

TOUDOUX: (*Beginning to give way.*) Now look... Think what you're asking... I haven't reached the age of thirty-eight to... Really! Now really! Really!

MME DE C: Never mind your age. (*Begging humbly.*) Be kind. Put it on. Put it on.

TOUDOUX: (*Weakening more and more.*) I mean to say...

LEONIE: (*Wailing feebly.*) Oh! I'm in agony.

MME DE C: (*Coaxing.*) Look, She's in agony. Julien... Put it on. Put it on.

TOUDOUX: (*As before.*) No. Listen, I... Anyway it doesn't fit me.

MME DE C: (*As before.*) How do you know? You haven't tried it.

TOUDOUX: I can see. It's not my size.

MME DE C: (*As before.*) Do put it on.

TOUDOUX: (*A final revolt.*) No, I couldn't...
(*He hesitates, goes to put it on, hesitates once or twice more, then, making a great decision, puts it on his head. Furiously.*) There! There! Are you satisfied? I've put it on. Are you satisfied?

MME DE C: (*Going to LEONIE, upstage beyond the card table.*) There, Leonie! He's a darling. He's put it on. He's put it on.

TOUDOUX: (*Squatting in front of the card table next to LEONIE so that she can see better; furiously.*) Yes, I have. Yes.

LEONIE: (*Raising her head from her arm and turning towards him.*) Show me. (*Looking at him.*) Oh!... How awful!

TOUDOUX: (*Dumbfounded.*) What!

LEONIE: (*Pushing him away.*) Go away. Go away. You look ridiculous.

TOUDOUX: (*Backing away.*) Me?

LEONIE: Get out of my sight. I'll never be able to see you again without that thing on your head.

TOUDOUX: Oh! She's impossible.

MME DE C: (*Having come downstage, pulling him by his left arm, so that he passes across.*) Stop annoying her. (*She goes upstage beyond the card table.*)

TOUDOUX: (*Exasperated.*) They don't care a damn about me.
(*CLEMENCE enters quickly from the hall and goes straight to the two women.*)

CLEMENCE: The midwife's here.

TOUDOUX: (*Furious.*) Send her away.

LEONIE and MME DE C: What!

CLEMENCE: (*Turning round at the sound of his voice and, finding herself with their noses almost touching, jumping at the dight of the chamber on his head.*) Oh!... Sir, you've gone mad!

LEONIE: 'Send her away'!

MME DE C: Send her in.

TOUDOUX: (*Raging.*) Send her in.

(*CLEMENCE goes out.*)

(*Returning to his old subject.*) How dare they play the fool with me! They ask me to put it on. I do so. (*Going to the card table opposite LEONIE.*) And instead of being grateful for my humiliating myself... (*As he speaks, he hits the table.*)

LEONIE: (*Unable to see anything but the chamber.*) Do take that thing off.

TOUDOUX: Oh? Well, I won't. I won't take it off. I've had enough of obeying your every whim. You wanted this? (*Tapping the bottom of the chamber.*) Well, I'll keep it. I don't change my mind the whole time even if you're weathercocks. (*He reaches the right.*)

LEONIE and MME DE C: Weathercocks!

(*MME VIRTUEL enters, followed by CLEMENCE who is carrying her bag. She comes downstage towards LEONIE, who has risen to receive her and with her mother's help moves to the chair at the right of the card table.*)

MME VIRTUEL: Good evening, ladies. (*She turns round towards TOUDOUX who, as he walks up and down, is coming back towards her.*) Good eve... (*Astonished at the sight of the chamber.*) Oh!

TOUDOUX: (*Curtly raising the chamber.*) Good evening. (*He goes upstage.*)

(*CLEMENCE, having put the bag on the floor, left of the armchair, goes out into the hall.*)

MME VIRTUEL: (*To TOUDOUX.*) You're in fancy dress?

TOUDOUX: (*Coming downstage towards her, raging.*) No, I am not. These ladies have cravings.

MME DE C: (*Quickly.*) Not me.

TOUDOUX: (*Removing the chamber.*) Here is a husband who put a chamber on his head to satisfy his wife's cravings.

MME VIRTUEL: (*Firmly.*) Ah! Splendid! What a good husband! Keep it on then. Keep it on.

TOUDOUX: Keep it on! Oh!... Oh!... I've had enough! (*TOUDOUX goes and puts the chamber on the floor, next to the console table and upstage of it. He then goes and sits in the armchair.*)

MME VIRTUEL: (*Having gone to LEONIE, who is sitting on the chair at the right of the card table.*) So you are the young mother-to-be?

LEONIE: Yes, I am. Yes.

MME DE C: (*Standing upstage of the table, between it and the back of LEONIE's chair.*) I don't think it will be long now, the contractions are happening quicker all the time.

MME VIRTUEL: Oh? Good. Good. Best to be rid of it as soon as possible. (*To LEONIE.*) Don't you agree?

LEONIE: Oh! Yes. Yes.

MME VIRTUEL: (*Taking off her gloves.*) I must say I didn't think it would be so soon. You wrote only yesterday to book me for next month... And my first visit coincides with your confinement.

LEONIE: I never dreamt I'd be one month early.

MME VIRTUEL: You haven't done anything silly?

LEONIE: Nothing.

MME VIRTUEL: Perhaps you made a mistake in the calculation?

LEONIE: That's impossible. We've only been married eight months.

MME DE C: (*Confirming.*) Eight months, yes.

MME VIRTUEL: And... (*Whispering, with a significant wink.*)... not before? Eh?

MME DE C: (*Scandalised.*) Oh!

LEONIE: (*Ashamed.*) Oh! Really! Oh!

MME VIRTUEL: (*Straightforward.*) No. No. I'm only asking to make sure.

LEONIE: (*As before.*) I understand, yes. (*Suddenly overcome with pain again.*) Oh! Oh! There it is again. Oh!

MME VIRTUEL: (*Firmly.*) Ah! That's good. That's good.

LEONIE: (*Bent double, rebelling.*) What do you mean, Good?

MME VIRTUEL: That shows it's coming along.

LEONIE: (*As before, furiously.*) Oh! I'd like to see you in this condition.

MME VIRTUEL: It's not all a bed of roses. I know, I've been through it. I've had two children and each time I was confined...

LEONIE: It's your job. You're used to it.

MME VIRTUEL: I'm used to it, yes. But not passively.

LEONIE: (*Her voice full of pain.*) Oh! Will it go on for long?

MME VIRTUEL: I can't say now. You must start getting ready. Go to your room. With your mother, she'll help put you to bed. I'll come and see you when you're there. In the meantime I'll do my unpacking. (*As she talks, she goes upstage a little, taking off her coat.*)

LEONIE: (*Rising.*) Yes.

MME DE C: (*Helping her to get up and taking her away.*) That's right. Come along, darling, come along.
(*LEONIE and MME DE CHAMPRINET go out. TOUDOUX rises. MME VIRTUEL, her coat under her arm, ignores him as if he didn't exist. She looks around the room, then, seeing the bellpush, left of the hall door, goes to it and rings. She then goes to the armchair for her bag and finds TOUDOUX standing in front of it, having followed her movements with his eyes from the beginning.*)

MME VIRTUEL: (*Without looking at him.*) Get out of my way.

TOUDOUX: (*Standing aside.*) Sorry.
(*MME VIRTUEL puts her coat down on the back of the armchair, opens her bag and takes out a jacket with the sleeves ready tucked up, an apron with a bib , and a case containing her equipment. She puts it all on the armchair, CLEMENCE enters from the pantry.*)

CLEMENCE: You rang, sir?

TOUDOUX: *She* did.

MME VIRTUEL: (*Sorting out her things on the armchair.*)
Yes, I did, The boiling water's ready?

CLEMENCE: The basins are on the stove.

MME VIRTUEL: Good. Everything's here from the chemist?

CLEMENCE: (*Pointing to the pantry.*) In there. Yes.

MME VIRTUEL: Good. Bring it along.
(*CLEMENCE goes out. MME VIRTUEL turns round,
holding her empty bag, and bumps into TOUDOUX.*)
Get out of my way.

TOUDOUX: (*Standing aside.*) Yes.

MME VIRTUEL: (*Thinking CLEMENCE is still there, as she
puts her open bag on the chair at the right of the card table.*)
Put it all on the mantelpiece.

TOUDOUX: (*Next to her.*) Who are you talking to?

MME VIRTUEL: (*Turning round.*) The maid.

TOUDOUX: She's gone.

MME VIRTUEL: Oh!... Right, I'll tell her when she comes
back. (*Finding him barring her path.*) Get out of my way.

TOUDOUX: (*Standing aside.*) Sorry.
(*MME VIRTUEL goes to the console table on the left of
which is a pile of towels. She takes one and spreads it out.
TOUDOUX has slowly reached her.*)

MME VIRTUEL: (*Turning round into him.*) You again!
Really! What are you here anyway?

TOUDOUX: (*Almost as an excuse.*) The husband.

MME VIRTUEL: The...... . Oh! Yes, of course, naturally,
you had the chamber. (*She has taken her case of equipment
from the armchair and spreads it out on the console table.*)

TOUDOUX: (*Dumbfounded.*) I had the...! (*Aside.*) Oh! I
can't stand much more. (*Trying to put himself into her good
graces.*) Hm... It... It must be exhausting being a midwife.

MME VIRTUEL: (*Curtly, without turning round.*) Yes.

TOUDOUX: Yes... Do you do a lot of confinements?

MME VIRTUEL: (*As before.*) Lots. Lots (*She comes downstage
in front of the armchair.*)

TOUDOUX: (*Pivoting, to come down after her.*) When you do
a confinement, do you...?

MME VIRTUEL: (*Cutting him short.*) Oh, no! No! You're not hoping I'll reveal my professional secrets, are you?

TOUDOUX: (*Submissively.*) No... No.

MME VIRTUEL: (*Taking off her hat and holding it out with her coat to TOUDOUX.*) Nobody's shown me where my room is. So take my hat and coat there, will you?

TOUDOUX: Me?

MME VIRTUEL: (*Putting them into his hands.*) Yes.

TOUDOUX: (*Submitting.*) Very well, (*He goes upstage, grumbling.*) It's unbelievable. Unbelievable!
(*TOUDOUX goes out into the hall. MME VIRTUEL reaches the right, undoing her bodice. As she has taken it off, CLEMENCE enters from the pantry carrying the medical equipment: big bottles of distilled water, yellow bottles of sublimate, packets of cotton wool, etc.*)

MME VIRTUEL: (*Surprised by her sudden entrance, starts and modestly crosses her hands on her chest.*) Who's there?

CLEMENCE: I'm bringing the medical things.

MME VIRTUEL: (*Reassured, reaching the armchair where she picks up her jacket.*) Ah! Good. Put them over there. (*She points to the console table.*)

CLEMENCE: (*Going downstage to the console table.*) Yes. (*She sets out the bottles and packets of cotton wool.*)
(*MME VIRTUEL gets ready to put on her jacket. TOUDOUX walks straight in from the hall.*)

TOUDOUX: That's done.

MME VIRTUEL: (*Left of the armchair, with a start.*) Don't come in.

TOUDOUX: (*Having gone round the dining table to come downstage left.*) Oh! Sorry, I didn't know.

MME VIRTUEL: (*Hurrying to put on her jacket with CLEMENCE's help.*) Can't you knock before you come in?

TOUDOUX: Yes, but I thought the dining room...

MME VIRTUEL: (*Furious.*) Never mind the dining room. (*Pulling the front of her jacket.*) My chest and shoulders were bare.

TOUDOUX: (*With a carefree gesture.*) Oh...

MME VIRTUEL: (*Having turned towards the armchair to get her apron, turning back as she puts it on and bumping into TOUDOUX, who has come near her.*) Now look here!... Am I going to have you under my feet all the time?

TOUDOUX: Oh! I can't help...

MME VIRTUEL: I can't stand having people about while I'm working. (*As she speaks, she takes her bodice from the armchair.*)

TOUDOUX: Oh! Oh!

MME VIRTUEL: (*Coming back holding the bodice and going towards her bag.*) Get out of my way.

TOUDOUX: Yes. (*He moves away.*)

MME VIRTUEL: (*Stuffing the bodice into the bag, which she then holds out to TOUDOUX.*) Take this to my room.

TOUDOUX: (*Taking it and holding it out to CLEMENCE.*) Clémence!

MME VIRTUEL: No, no! Not Clémence. If I'd wanted Clémence to do it, I'd have told her. I need her here.

TOUDOUX: (*Taken aback.*) Oh!

MME VIRTUEL: Yes.

TOUDOUX: (*Submitting.*) All right. (*Grumbling, as he goes out.*) Oh!... Damnation!... (*He goes out.*)

MME VIRTUEL: (*Adjusting the bib of her apron with safety pins.*) Now my girl, go and see if your water's boiling. When it's ready, bring me a basin in the bedroom, so I've got it handy. (*She reaches the left.*)

CLEMENCE: (*She finishes setting everything out on the console.*) Very good.
(*A knock at the hall door.*)

MME VIRTUEL: Come in.
(*TOUDOUX enters and comes downstage centre.*)
Was that you knocking?

TOUDOUX: Yes, of course.

MME VIRTUEL: Why do you have to knock, now I'm dressed?

TOUDOUX: I couldn't know. I didn't look through the keyhole.

MME VIRTUEL: (*Sceptical.*) Yes!

TOUDOUX: (*With a trace of bitterness.*) You've nothing more for me to do?

MME VIRTUEL: (*Dismissing him with a gesture.*) No, no. I don't need you for anything. Get out of my way. (*She moves to the centre.*)

CLEMENCE: What about me?

MME VIRTUEL: No. What time do you have dinner?

TOUDOUX: We've had it.

MME VIRTUEL: Already? I haven't.

TOUDOUX: Oh!

MME VIRTUEL: Naturally. I was just going to sit down, when you sent for me. Well! There's nothing to eat?

TOUDOUX: You're hungry?

MME VIRTUEL: You don't eat because you're hungry. You eat because it's time to.

TOUDOUX: Oh! There must be something left. (*To CLEMENCE.*) Eh?

CLEMENCE: Yes, sir.

MME VIRTUEL: What sort of soup did you have?

CLEMENCE: We didn't.

MME VIRTUEL: (*Looking at her and making a face.*) That's not much of a meal.

TOUDOUX: We never eat it.

MME VIRTUEL: (*Turning towards him.*) I do.

TOUDOUX: Oh!

MME VIRTUEL: Yes.

TOUDOUX: (*Bowing.*) Good.

MME VIRTUEL: Yes. Oh, I know! That's the fashion today. (*Simpering, screwing up her mouth.*) We don't eat soup any more! (*Firmly.*) I'm the old school. The good school. I don't believe in progress.

TOUDOUX: Aha!

MME VIRTUEL: (*In the same tone as before, as if continuing.*) What next?

TOUDOUX: (*Conciliating.*) Yes. What next?... Nothing.

MME VIRTUEL: What! No soup! And then nothing!

TOUDOUX: (*Realising his mistake.*) Eh? Oh! No. Yes. Yes... No. I thought you were saying you don't believe in progress, what next?

MME VIRTUEL: No, no. Next after the soup?

TOUDOUX: Ah! After the soup, yes, yes. Well! After the... after the soup... after the soup we haven't had! Roast veal and macaroni.

MME VIRTUEL: (*Nodding.*) And after that?

TOUDOUX: That's all.

MME VIRTUEL: (*With a pout.*) That's not much.

CLEMENCE: A piece of Roquefort.

MME VIRTUEL: That doesn't count.

(*CLEMENCE goes upstage beyond the table and picks up MME DE CHAMPRINET's coat.*)

You've small stomachs here.

TOUDOUX: Well...

MME VIRTUEL: (*Going towards the dining table.*) I'll have that, as it's all there is.

(*She sits left of the table.*)

CLEMENCE: (*Upstage of the table, carefully folding the coat.*) What will you drink? White wine? Or red?

MME VIRTUEL: (*Casually.*) Oh, anything. I don't mind... A little champagne.

TOUDOUX: (*In front of the table.*) Champagne?

MME VIRTUEL: Yes. It's best for my stomach.

TOUDOUX: That's what you drink at home?

MME VIRTUEL: (*With meaning.*) When my clients send me some.

TOUDOUX: Oh!

MME VIRTUEL: Yes.

TOUDOUX: (*Submitting.*) Good. (*To CLEMENCE who is upstage right of the table.*) Go down to the grocer's and get some sparkling wine, you know...

CLEMENCE: There's no need to. We've a bottle of Pommery left. (*She goes towards the pantry door.*)

MME VIRTUEL: (*Good natured.*) That's right.

TOUDOUX: (*Furious, coming downstage right.*) Damn the girl!

MME VIRTUEL: Pommery! I don't mind. I'll make do with that. I only drink one bottle.

TOUDOUX: (*Ironically.*) Really?

MME VIRTUEL: (*Munching a piece of bread.*) I don't want to be any bother.

TOUDOUX: How thoughtful!

CLEMENCE: (*Picking up the empty wine bottle from the table.*) When shall I serve dinner?

MME VIRTUEL: (*Rising and coming downstage.*) When it's ready. Heat it up and serve it then.

CLEMENCE: It will take about ten minutes.

MME VIRTUEL: We've lots of time. (*She sits right of the card table.*)
(*CLEMENCE goes out with the bottle and MME DE CHAMPRINET's coat.*)
The baby's not due yet.

TOUDOUX: (*Going towards her.*) Oh! Will it be long?

MME VIRTUEL: Well... If she's primiparous!

TOUDOUX: (*Frowning, not understanding.*) If she's...

MME VIRTUEL: Primiparous... Then it's not so quick. Your wife is primiparous?

TOUDOUX: (*Spreading out his arms, not knowing how to answer.*) Well...

MME VIRTUEL: Is she primiparous or multiparous? *TOUDOUX makes a face. A pause.*

TOUDOUX: (*After waving his hands, as if to say 'between the two'. Sharply and decisively.*) Viviparous.

MME VIRTUEL: (*Astounded.*) What! (*Laughing.*) Of course she's viviparous. We're all viviparous.

TOUDOUX: That's right, we're all viviparous.

MME VIRTUEL: Not you.

TOUDOUX: Not me, no, not me.

MME VIRTUEL: You haven't told me if she's primiparous.

TOUDOUX: (*Hesitating.*) Well... (*Decisively.*) No.

MME VIRTUEL: Ah! Good. It will be quicker. How many children has she had?

TOUDOUX: (*Decisively as before.*) None.

MME VIRTUEL: Well, then! She's primiparous.

TOUDOUX: That's right. She's primiparous.

MME VIRTUEL: Well, then! That's all I'm asking. (*She rises.*)

TOUDOUX: I didn't quite hear the question.

MME VIRTUEL: (*Going upstage, right of the table, towards LEONIE's door.*) Now! Let's have a peep at our patient.

TOUDOUX: (*Following on her heels.*) If you're ready, let's.

MME VIRTUEL: (*Turning round so sharply that TOUDOUX bumps into her.*) Oh, no... No! Not you! You stay here! I don't want anyone.

TOUDOUX: Oh!

MME VIRTUEL: Anyone. Anyone. When I'm delivering, husbands and lovers... out!

TOUDOUX: Lovers! My wife has no lovers!

MME VIRTUEL: I don't say she has. I say husbands and lovers I will not have, that's final. (*On the last word, she makes a half turn into the doorway.*)

TOUDOUX: Yes, but...

MME VIRTUEL: (*Turning round quickly. Commandingly.*) Stay here.
(*MME VIRTUEL goes out into LEONIE's bedroom. The bell rings.*)

TOUDOUX: Oh! That woman's maddening!
(*CLEMENCE enters from the pantry with a basin of water. Hearing the bell, she hesitates whether to continue with the basin or open the door.*)

CLEMENCE: Do you mind opening the door, sir, I'm busy with the water?

TOUDOUX: Is no-one else in the kitchen?

CLEMENCE: No, sir, and I must take the basin in.
(*Bell rings.*)

TOUDOUX: To my wife's room? You can't. They don't want anyone, not even me.

CLEMENCE: Yes, but I...
(*Bell rings. Neither of them takes any notice.*)
Do you mind knocking, my hands are full.

TOUDOUX: (*Sceptical.*) Yes, all right, but... (*He knocks.*)

MME VIRTUEL: (*Off.*) Don't come in.

TOUDOUX: (*Triumphant.*) There!
(*Bell rings.*)

CLEMENCE: (*Unruffled.*) It's me, the maid.

MME VIRTUEL: (*Off.*) Oh, it's you. Come in.

CLEMENCE: (*Her turn to be triumphant.*) There!
  (*Bell rings. CLEMENCE goes out into LEONIE's room.*)
TOUDOUX: (*Reaching the right.*) Charming! That's
  charming!
  (*Bell rings.*)
  Yes! All right!
  (*TOUDOUX goes out into the hall. The stage is empty for a
  moment.*)
DE CHAMPRINET: (*Off.*) Well! I've been here for hours!
TOUDOUX: (*Off.*) I can't help it. I have to answer
  the door.
  (*DE CHAMPRINET enters, hat on head, cane in hand,
  followed by TOUDOUX.*)
DE CHAMPRINET: (*As he enters.*) Oh, no! No! Really!
  Dammit, no!
TOUDOUX: I can't help it.
DE CHAMPRINET: (*Extreme left.*) I'm furious. I can never
  get five minutes peace.
TOUDOUX: Yes...
DE CHAMPRINET: I don't know how you manage,
  dammit!
TOUDOUX: It's not my fault.
DE CHAMPRINET: (*Raising his hat.*) It's not mine either.
  (*Putting his hat on again.*) I was sitting quietly at the club,
  having my usual game of écarté before dinner... at a
  hundred francs a game. I was in luck too. Then, bang,
  I get the news... straight in the guts. Very amusing! Of
  course I stopped. (*He sits at the left of the card table, takes his
  hat off and puts it on the table.*) What do you expect?
  I know my duty. But really, if they can't let you have a
  moment's rest at the end of the day...
TOUDOUX: (*Seated at the right of the table.*) I'm very sorry.
DE CHAMPRINET: (*Rising, picking up his hat and putting
  it on.*) A lot of use that is! (*Going towards the door of
  LEONIE's room.*) Well! Can I see my daughter?
TOUDOUX: At the moment she's in the hands of the
  midwife... who's not exactly easy.

DE CHAMPRINET: (*Grumbling.*) Oh!... (*Taking his hat off and putting it and his cane on the chair at the left of the dining table.*) Anyway you can give me something to eat. With all this, I've had no dinner. (*He reaches the right.*)

TOUDOUX: (*Still seated.*) Do you mind making do with what there is?

DE CHAMPRINET: I'm not hungry. Naturally all this has completely taken away my appetite.
(*CLEMENCE enters from LEONIE's room.*)

TOUDOUX: Ah, Clémence! Will you lay another place for Monsieur de Champrinet?

CLEMENCE: Very good, sir.
(*CLEMENCE takes de CHAMPRINET's hat and cane and goes out.*)

DE CHAMPRINET: (*Having pricked up his ears.*) Another place? You've got company?

TOUDOUX: Yes.

DE CHAMPRINET: Oh?

TOUDOUX: The midwife.

DE CHAMPRINET: (*Annoyed.*) Aha! I'm having dinner with the midwife?

TOUDOUX: Well...

DE CHAMPRINET: (*As before.*) Yes, all right. All right. Oh!

TOUDOUX: Just this once.

DE CHAMPRINET: (*Upstage of the card table.*) Yes, yes. (*Grumbling.*) The midwife! (*Sitting at the left of the card table opposite TOUDOUX.*) What the devil have you been up to, bringing it on today? You weren't expecting it for another month.

TOUDOUX: Léonie's early.

DE CHAMPRINET: (*Automatically picking up the cards and shuffling them.*) That's very amusing. A child after being married eight months! What will people think? No one will believe it.

TOUDOUX: Oh! Well...

DE CHAMPRINET: They'll start hinting you had a little something on account. Nobody in Society could under-

stand why a de Champrinet should marry his daughter
to a Toudoux. Obviously now they'll say I had to. Very
pleasant!

TOUDOUX: (*Upset.*) Women are often a month early.

DE CHAMPRINET: Of course they are. This proves it.
(*Dealing the cards for écarté.*) They are. But not in
Society. The way you do things!... (*Picking up his hand.*)
Your lead.

TOUDOUX: (*Seated facing the audience, automatically picking
up his hand.*) If you had to care about what people
say... (*Leading.*)... in Society! Spades!

DE CHAMPRINET: Of course you have to. I've the
king... I'll be furious... I trump that... if they say my
daughter... Trump, trump... had a baby after eight
months... King of diamonds, queen of hearts... King,
I've got the lot. Three points. (*Pushing the cards over to
TOUDOUX.*) Your deal... You can laugh at what
people think...

TOUDOUX: (*Shuffling the cards.*) Oh... (*He passes them
across.*)

DE CHAMPRINET: (*Cutting them.*) You can laugh, but
you can't ignore it.

TOUDOUX: (*Dealing.*) If you always had to mind what
people say!

DE CHAMPRINET: (*Picking up his hand.*) Of course you
have to. Hearts.... I've the king... (*He leads.*)

TOUDOUX: Yes, oh... I trump.

DE CHAMPRINET: There! The whole thing's infuriating.
(*TOUDOUX having led.*) I trump... Trump, trump and
trump... I've won... You owe me a hundred francs.

TOUDOUX: (*Remaining open mouthed with his last card in the
air.*) I owe you...? I wasn't playing.

DE CHAMPRINET: Not playing? What were you doing?

TOUDOUX: I was playing, yes, but not for a hundred francs.

DE CHAMPRINET: Marvellous! You might have said so!

TOUDOUX: *You* should have.

DE CHAMPRINET: I always play for a hundred francs.
I told you just now. If you'd won, I'd have paid up.

TOUDOUX: Maybe, but that's no reason why I should, when I've lost.

DE CHAMPRINET: (*Rising and going upstage.*) This is too much... Right! I won't play another game.

TOUDOUX: Do you think I feel like playing?

DE CHAMPRINET: Eh? (*Firmly.*) Nor do I. I played automatically. I'd never have dreamt of it with my poor daughter going through such agony.

TOUDOUX: (*Rising and going towards LEONIE's door, followed by DE CHAMPRINET.*) And for so long!... What on earth can they be doing in there? (*They both put their ears to the door.*)

DE CHAMPRINET: Yes. I must say I'd like to give my daughter a kiss,
(*MME VIRTUEL enters quickly, backwards, with a basin of water and turns round straight into TOUDOUX, who is upstage of her, soaking him. DE CHAMPRINET escapes by moving back.*)

TOUDOUX: (*Leaping back.*) Ohhh!

MME VIRTUEL: (*Reaching midstage.*) Well, well! Just look at that! Well, well!

TOUDOUX: This is the limit. You not only soak me...

MME VIRTUEL: That's your bad luck. You shouldn't be under my feet the whole time.

TOUDOUX: (*Coming downstage extreme left.*) I'm drenched!

MME VIRTUEL: That will teach the pair of you not to look through the keyhole.

DE CHAMPRINET: (*Not believing his ears.*) What!

TOUDOUX: (*Protesting.*) Keyhole!

DE CHAMPRINET: Really...!

TOUDOUX: (*Reaching centre stage.*) We do not look through keyholes.

MME VIRTUEL: (*Sceptical.*) Oh...

TOUDOUX: Now I'll have to go and change.

MME VIRTUEL: (*Who has been looking for somewhere to put her basin, turning round.*) Then be useful for once. Take this basin to the kitchen as you go. (*She thrusts it into his hands.*)

TOUDOUX: Me!

MME VIRTUEL: Run along.

TOUDOUX: (*Moving away with the basin, furious.*) Ohhh! What a woman!

(*TOUDOUX goes out.*)

DE CHAMPRINET: I say! I'd like to see my daughter.

MME VIRTUEL: You'll have to wait. I don't need strangers now. (*She sits in the armchair.*)

DE CHAMPRINET: Strangers! I'm her father.

MME VIRTUEL: You're a stranger at the confinement.

DE CHAMPRINET: (*Bowing.*) Oh...

MME VIRTUEL: All right. In a moment I'll allow you to kiss your little girl.

DE CHAMPRINET: Little girl! She's a married woman!

MME VIRTUEL: That may be. To you she'll always be a little girl. You may kiss her, but go straight into the room and out again. In the meantime I'll go and tell your lady you're here, in case she chooses to see you. Get out of my way. (*She passes in front of him and goes towards LEONIE's door.*)

DE CHAMPRINET: I must say, you're not exactly charming.

MME VIRTUEL: (*Coming back towards him.*) Charming! Charming!... I'm not a cocotte!

DE CHAMPRINET: What!

MME VIRTUEL: I'm past the age for dilly-dallying with men.

DE CHAMPRINET: I'm not asking you to dilly-dally.

MME VIRTUEL: You're doing much the same. When I'm working, my mind's on my job. At other times I can laugh all right.

DE CHAMPRINET: (*Mockingly.*) Ah!

MME VIRTUEL: But when the bugle sounds... (*Striking her chest.*) I'm ready.

DE CHAMPRINET: Ah! Good. Good. Carry on.

MME VIRTUEL: Yes. (*She turns round and goes towards the door.*)

DE CHAMPRINET: (*Theatrically.*) Gird up your loins!

MME VIRTUEL: (*Turning round sharply: with dignity.*) I beg your pardon!

DE CHAMPRINET: No! It's a figure of speech.

MME VIRTUEL: (*As before.*) Oh!... So I should hope... I'll send in your lady.

DE CHAMPRINET: (*Going to the right of the card table and sitting.*) That's right.

(*MME VIRTUEL goes out.*)

(*Picking up the cards.*) Oh, damn!... Damn, damn, damn, damn, damn, damn! (*Dealing the cards, as if playing écarté with an imaginary partner.*) 'Not a cocotte'! I believe her. (*Calling trumps.*) Spades.

(*He puts down the pack, picks up his hand and looks at it for a moment; then he puts it on the table, picks up his opponent's hand, looks at it and puts it down with a hollow laugh.*) He has the king. (*He picks up his hand again, is about to lead, then, changing his mind, picks up the other hand again, removes the king, puts it in his own hand and gives the other a low card in exchange.*) His lead.

(*MME DE CHAMPRINET enters from LEONIE's room.*)

MME DE C: You're alone?

DE CHAMPRINET: Yes. Toudoux's gone to change his trousers.

MME DE C: He cares about his appearance when his wife's on her bed of suffering!

DE CHAMPRINET: He was soaked by the midwife. How is she?

MME DE C: (*Sitting at the left of the card table.*) Who? The midwife?

DE CHAMPRINET: No, Léonie. I don't care a damn about the midwife.

MME DE C: It's running its course.

DE CHAMPRINET: Oh! Oh, yes. This is just what we needed! I've been in a fury for the last hour. A baby!... After being married eight months! (*He rises.*)

MME DE C: Yes, it's very upsetting.

DE CHAMPRINET: There's your Toudoux for you! That's what your Toudoux does!

MME DE C: My Toudoux! He's not my Toudoux.

DE CHAMPRINET: (*Reaching midstage right.*) You insisted on this marriage. I didn't want it.

MME DE C: You didn't want any husband, Toudoux or anyone else. You hated him before you met him.

DE CHAMPRINET: (*Having gone upstage of the card table.*) I can't help that. I think the man's disgusting. We've only one daughter and to bring her up properly, we sacrificed everything. Then, bang, suddenly, there's a man, a man... we don't know. (*Coming downstage a little.*) And that's that!... He takes your daughter away and sleeps with her. (*Hammering the table with his fist.*) And we know. We accept it. (*Sitting at the right of the card table.*) Don't you think it's disgusting?

MME DE C: What do you expect? That's marriage.

DE CHAMPRINET: (*Facing the audience, his left arm on the back of his chair.*) All right, I know it is. (*Looking at the door through which TOUDOUX went out.*) Her Toudoux! Her Toudoux! (*Turning his head towards his wife.*) Do you like the man?

MME DE C: Really...

DE CHAMPRINET: (*Looking towards the door again.*) Ohhh! If I had to sleep with him, I couldn't.

MME DE C: (*Mockingly.*) He never asked you to marry him!

DE CHAMPRINET: Oh! If he had!

MME DE C: Anyway he makes your daughter happy.

DE CHAMPRINET: (*Rising.*) That's the last straw.

MME DE C: He's very kind. Let's be fair to him behind his back. He's so willing to comply with her whims. I saw that just now. Léonie had such a craving! As a pregnant woman does.

DE CHAMPRINET: He satisfied it? He only did his duty.

MME DE C: Even so, I know men who... She insisted on him putting a chamber pot on his head.

DE CHAMPRINET: (*Not daring to believe such a godsend, sitting at the right of the card table.*) And... he did?

MME DE C: (*Separating the words.*) He... did.

DE CHAMPRINET: (*Feasting on it.*) How marvellous! That does make me happy. My son-in-law with a chamber on his head! I'm delighted.

MME DE C: You wicked man!

DE CHAMPRINET: (*As before, picking up the cards.*) Why not? I can't stand the sight of him. Your lead.

MME DE C: What?

DE CHAMPRINET: (*His eyes on the ceiling.*) I've the king.

MME DE C: You've the king! I'm not playing écarté!

DE CHAMPRINET: (*Taken aback.*) Eh? (*Protesting.*) I'm not either. I said I'd the king, because I have the king. Without thinking. I've so much on my mind.

MME DE C: No more than me, I assure you.

(*TOUDOUX enters from the hall.*)

TOUDOUX: I've had to change every stitch.

DE CHAMPRINET: Ah, there you are.

TOUDOUX: Here I am, yes.

(*MME VIRTUEL bursts in from LEONIE's room.*)

MME VIRTUEL: The young lady wants her mummy and daddy.

DE CHAMPRINET: Ah!

(*DE CHAMPRINET and his wife rise simultaneously.*)

MME VIRTUEL: (*Quickly barring his way, as he rushes forward first.*) Just for a moment, you know. Just for a moment.

DE CHAMPRINET: (*Pushing her to his left, so that she goes upstage right of the card table.*) Yes, yes.

MME VIRTUEL: (*Rubbing her right shoulder.*) Oh! He's hurt me.

DE CHAMPRINET: (*In the doorway, to his wife who is following.*) That old woman gets on my nerves.

MME VIRTUEL: I've been assaulted.

MME DE C: Here's your father, my sweet.

(*MME DE CHAMPRINET goes out.*)

DE CHAMPRINET: (*As he goes out.*) Well, my darling, how are you?

(*DE CHAMPRINET goes out. TOUDOUX goes towards MME VIRTUEL, who is sitting at the right of the card table and beginning to tell her fortune with the cards.*)

TOUDOUX: Is it coming along a little?

MME VIRTUEL: (*Bleating voice, without turning round, as she makes up two packs of cards and cuts the bottom one.*) Mm!

TOUDOUX: Nothing much yet?

MME VIRTUEL: Pooh!... She's got to twenty sous. (*She bends her forefinger round to her thumb, to make an opening the size of a twenty sous coin.*)

TOUDOUX: (*Without understanding.*) Ah! She's...

MME VIRTUEL: And when I say twenty sous, I'm exaggerating.

TOUDOUX: Ah!

MME VIRTUEL: She's between ten *and* twenty.

TOUDOUX: (*Wanting to appear to understand.*) Yes, I see, she's got to fifteen sous.

MME VIRTUEL: (*Turning round sharply.*) Fifteen sous! What do you mean, fifteen sous? That's money, not a size.

TOUDOUX: (*Intimidated.*) Oh! Ah! Yes, yes... Of course that's... that's money.

MME VIRTUEL: No... like this. (*She bends her finger round to her thumb as before.*)

TOUDOUX: (*No better off.*) Like that. Yes... It's... not serious?

MME VIRTUEL: No... No. But it won't happen right away.

TOUDOUX: Oh! Yes... There's nothing wrong?

MME VIRTUEL: No, no. (*Rising.*) Though there are things I don't understand.

TOUDOUX: Oh!

MME VIRTUEL: I've felt the young mother-to-be and I can't make out anything definite.

TOUDOUX: Aha!

MME VIRTUEL: (*Casually.*) There might be a slight hydramnios.

TOUDOUX: (*Not having understood a word, but not wanting to give that impression.*) That wouldn't surprise me, no.

MME VIRTUEL: At the same time I thought I could feel three firm areas. (*With her forefinger she hits him in the stomach three times in succession, right, left, right.*)

TOUDOUX: Well?

MME VIRTUEL: I don't know. (*Sitting down again at right of card table.*) It might be an ingeminate pregnancy.

TOUDOUX: (*Leaning towards her, frowning as if he had not heard properly.*) Ingem...?

MME VIRTUEL: ...inate. (*Leaning back against the table, her left arm on the back of her chair.*) Do you know of any previous cases of ingeminate births in your family or hers?
(*TOUDOUX slowly spreads out his arms and sinks his neck into his shoulders to show he doesn't know.*)
You don't remember? No?

TOUDOUX: Well...

MME VIRTUEL: Yes, you don't remember.

TOUDOUX: No, no, I don't... What can that lead to?

MME VIRTUEL: What can that...? (*Rising.*) Twins.

TOUDOUX: (*With a start.*) Twins! (*Reaching the right.*) Good heavens! Two cradles! Two prams!

MME VIRTUEL: (*Reaching the left.*) Well, I say that. But without a stethoscope of course. (*Sitting at the left of the card table.*) Do you know if they've used a stethoscope?

TOUDOUX: (*Standing at the right of the card table.*) Stetho...?

MME VIRTUEL: ...scope.

TOUDOUX: (*Hesitating.*) Ah! No... No. (*Sitting down.*) She had a bath this morning.

MME VIRTUEL: That has nothing to do with it. It's like me asking if you get colds and you saying no, you wear elastic braces. (*Rising.*) It's as stupid as that.

TOUDOUX: Oh! Sorry.

MME VIRTUEL: (*Upstage of the card table.*) I'm asking if they've used a stethoscope on her, as that would give an indication of the heartbeats.

TOUDOUX: Yes, yes.

MME VIRTUEL: (*Casually, as if she were talking about the most usual matters.*) It may be simply a left sacro posterior, with a detached placenta, breach presentation.

TOUDOUX: Breach presentation?

MME VIRTUEL: Yes. (*She goes upstage to the dining table, where she looks for a piece of bread.*)

TOUDOUX: (*Seizing her bottom with his right hand, thus bringing her back to him.*) I say!... Er... Madam What's your name!

MME VIRTUEL: (*Held.*) Ohhh!

TOUDOUX: Breach presentation... Is that good?

MME VIRTUEL: (*Upstage of the card table, nibbling her piece of bread.*) Well... I'd prefer a vertex.

TOUDOUX: A vertex. Ah, yes, a vertex, of course.

MME VIRTUEL: Clearly a right or left occipito, anterior or posterior...

TOUDOUX: Yes, yes. Never mind.

MME VIRTUEL: (*Reaching the armchair as she speaks.*) Ah, you see strange things in our profession. (*Sitting.*) The other day I actually had a patient who produced a hydatidiform mole.

TOUDOUX: Really.

MME VIRTUEL: (*With an impressive gesture.*) A bunch of grapes, you know.

TOUDOUX: (*Copying her.*) of course, a bunch of grapes.

MME VIRTUEL: (*Settling into the armchair.*) I'm sure you haven't often seen that.

TOUDOUX: No... No. I don't remember... (*Aside.*) Ohhh! She's driving me mad with her technical terms.

MME VIRTUEL: A hydatidiform mole's very odd, very odd.

TOUDOUX: Ah, yes. Yes, it's... (*Rising and going towards her.*) Well, I've never seen a... hydatidiform mole, but I have seen... a case of... you may not know...

MME VIRTUEL: (*Importantly, without hesitation.*) of course I know.

TOUDOUX: (*His hand on the back of the armchair.*) A case of... (*Very slowly.*) mistamboulocolitis.

MME VIRTUEL: (*Sitting forward.*) What?

TOUDOUX: (*Categorically.*) Mistamboulocolitis.

MME VIRTUEL: (*Apparently racking her brains for a moment, then sinking back into her chair.*) Ah, yes, yes, that does happen.

TOUDOUX: (*Dumbfounded.*) You've seen it?

MME VIRTUEL: Lots of times.

TOUDOUX: (*Reaching midstage left.*) How dare she?

MME VIRTUEL: (*To change the subject.*) Aren't we going to have dinner?

TOUDOUX: (*Going towards the pantry door.*) I think so, yes.

MME VIRTUEL: (*Rising and going upstage towards the dining table.*) I'm starving.

TOUDOUX: (*Into the wings, having opened the pantry door.*) Clémence! You can serve dinner.
DE CHAMPRINET enters from LEONIE's room.

MME VIRTUEL: Ah! There you are!

DE CHAMPRINET: Yes.

MME VIRTUEL: (*Reprimanding him.*) I said straight in and out again. You're irresponsible.

DE CHAMPRINET: Oh!

MME VIRTUEL: Irresponsible.

DE CHAMPRINET: (*Standing with one knee on chair right of the card table.*) All right, I am. Tell me... I've seen the poor girl, she's very brave. Will this go on for long?

MME VIRTUEL: (*With a vague gesture.*) Well... (*She goes upstage to the dining table.*)

TOUDOUX: (*Happy to show off his knowledge, casually.*) She's got to twenty sous.

DE CHAMPRINET: (*After looking at him with astonishment.*) What does that mean?

TOUDOUX: (*With a sudden shout of triumph, smacking MME VIRTUEL's bottom, as she stands with her back to the audience, busy rummaging about at the dining table.*) Ah!

MME VIRTUEL: (*Turning round with a start.*) Oh!

TOUDOUX: Ah! You don't know either. I'm delighted. Madam What's-her-name there.

MME VIRTUEL: (*Shocked.*) 'What's-her-name'!

TOUDOUX: Virtuel.

DE CHAMPRINET: What does he mean, got to twenty sous?

MME VIRTUEL: Eh?... Well, you see, it's when the...
(*She vaguely sketches an explanatory gesture, then changes her mind.*) No. No. These things are not for children.
(*Wagging a finger under his chin, as if to a baby.*) Diddums. Diddums, diddums. (*She goes to the left, pushes the chair at the right of the card table under it, in order to free the view of the dining table for the following scenes, then goes*

round the card table upstage and comes downstage
extreme left.)

DE CHAMPRINET: (*After remaining for a moment taken
aback, going to TOUDOUX, who is in front of the armchair,
his hands on his hips.*) She's laughing at me.

TOUDOUX: She is a character.

(*CLEMENCE enters with the remains of the meat and a
dish full of macaroni, together with the bottle of Pommery,
which she puts on the table.*)

CLEMENCE: Dinner is served. (*She puts the food on the
sideboard.*)

MME VIRTUEL: Ah! (*She goes quickly to DE CHAMPRINET
who is still in the same position and puts his arm in hers.*)

DE CHAMPRINET: (*Surprised, turning his head towards her.*)
What is it?

MME VIRTUEL: I'm taking your arm. Dinner's served.

DE CHAMPRINET: (*With ironically exaggerated politeness.*)
Oh! I'm sorry.

MME VIRTUEL: The two of us dining alone! It's like an
assignment.

DE CHAMPRINET: (*Bowing; mockingly.*) As you say, an
assignment. (*They go upstage. TOUDOUX sits in the armchair.*)

MME VIRTUEL: Where will you sit?

DE CHAMPRINET: (*Very courteous.*) Wherever you don't
wish to.

MME VIRTUEL: (*Moving to left, pointing to the chair on the
left.*) Then I'll sit here, so I won't get the draught from
the door in my back.

DE CHAMPRINET: (*Bowing, as if honoured.*) Thank you.
(*They sit down, facing each other. In the meantime
CLEMENCE has been laying the table, taking new cutlery
etc. from the sideboard.*)

MME VIRTUEL: Now, my girl, while I'm eating, you go
into the bedroom. In case the patient needs anyone...

CLEMENCE: What about serving?

MME VIRTUEL: We'll manage. If we need anything,
(*Pointing to TOUDOUX, who is still seated.*) he's had
dinner, he can hand it round.

TOUDOUX: Me!

MME VIRTUEL: Anyway there isn't much. You can put it all on the table.

DE CHAMPRINET: Yes, no need to be formal.

CLEMENCE: (*Putting the food on the table.*) Very good. (*She goes towards LEONIE's door.*)

MME VIRTUEL: (*Graciously to TOUDOUX.*) There's nothing like service by men.

TOUDOUX: (*Bowing; ironically.*) You're too kind.
(*CLEMENCE knocks at the door.*)

MME DE C: (*Off.*) Come in.
(*CLEMENCE goes out.*)

MME VIRTUEL: (*Falling back into her chair; flirtatiously.*) Ah! This is nice.

DE CHAMPRINET: (*Helping himself to meat.*) What is?

MME VIRTUEL: Here. The two of us.

DE CHAMPRINET: (*Ironically.*) Ah! Yes.

MME VIRTUEL: (*Helping herself to macaroni.*) I remember having a little party like this with the Duc de Cussinge... (*Passing him the dish.*) Help yourself.

DE CHAMPRINET: Thank you. (*He does so.*)

MME VIRTUEL: ...when the Duchess was confined.

DE CHAMPRINET: Oh, you did the...

MME VIRTUEL: (*Swallowing a mouthful of macaroni.*) I did, yes. It happened through my intermittence. (*She eats.*)

DE CHAMPRINET: (*Repeating deliberately.*) Your intermittence? Did it?

MME VIRTUEL: We had supper... alone together... like this, with the Duke. (*Flirtatiously.*) He's a one!

DE CHAMPRINET: Is he indeed?

MME VIRTUEL: Like here this evening. Apart from a mass of flunkeys.

TOUDOUX: (*Mockingly, from the same place.*) I apologise.

MME VIRTUEL: I wasn't blaming you. I haven't any at home. (*She eats.*)

TOUDOUX: Ah!... Good.

MME VIRTUEL: (*Holding out the champagne.*) Here, open the champagne.

TOUDOUX: Me?

MME VIRTUEL: Of course, you.

TOUDOUX: (*Rising.*) Yes... Yes, yes. (*He takes it and goes and sits on the chair against the wall at the right of LEONIE's door.*)

MME VIRTUEL: (*Looking at DE CHAMPRINET.*) Why, de Cussinge, de Champrinet, it's like comrade and companion. Are you an aristocrat too?

DE CHAMPRINET: (*Modest.*) Well...

MME VIRTUEL: What are you? Marquis? Viscount? What?

DE CHAMPRINET: (*As before.*) Count.

MME VIRTUEL: (*Appreciatively.*) Ah! Count. Good... if you're a count, how do you come to have a son-in-law... (*She turns towards TOUDOUX, who is still trying to open the bottle.*) ...who's a nobody?

DE CHAMPRINET: Well... you can't always choose.

MME VIRTUEL: (*Eating.*) I do agree.

TOUDOUX: Charming, they are!

MME VIRTUEL: (*In a choked voice.*) Oh, this macaroni's heavy. Isn't it?

DE CHAMPRINET: (*Similarly.*) I was just thinking the same thing.

MME VIRTUEL: (*Getting hiccups.*) Hic!... Oh, I've got the hicks. Hic!... Haven't you?

DE CHAMPRINET: No, I never get hiccups.

MME VIRTUEL: Lucky you! Hic! (*Turning round towards TOUDOUX.*) Do hurry up with that bottle... hic... you!

TOUDOUX: I can't get the cork out, it's stuck.

MME VIRTUEL: (*Upturning the empty jug.*) How delightful! There's... hic... not even any water... Hic!

DE CHAMPRINET: I must say... hic... I'm thirsty. Good heavens... hic... I've hiccups too.

MME VIRTUEL: Do try a cork... hic... screw.

DE CHAMPRINET: (*Rising.*) Come on. Give it.. hic.. to me.

TOUDOUX: (*Going towards him.*) With pleasure. I hope you can manage it.

MME VIRTUEL: (*Coming downstage.*) Hurry up... Hic!

DE CHAMPRINET: Yes, yes... Hic!

(*TOUDOUX is standing centre stage between DE CHAMPRINET, who is trying to open the bottle,*

and MME VIRTUEL, who is impatient to see it opened.
DE CHAMPRINET and MME VIRTUEL have hiccups
alternately, as if answering each other.)

MME VIRTUEL: Hic!
   (*A pause.*)
DE CHAMPRINET: Hic!
   (*A pause.*)
MME VIRTUEL: Hic!
   (*A pause.*)
DE CHAMPRINET: Hic!
   (*A pause.*)
MME VIRTUEL: (*Getting impatient.*) Hic!... Oh!
   (*A pause.*)
DE CHAMPRINET: Hic!
   (*A pause.*)
MME VIRTUEL and DE CHAMPRINET: (*Together.*) Hic!
   (*A pause.*)
TOUDOUX: (*Coming downstage left.*) It's maddening when
   other people have hiccups and you haven't.
DE CHAMPRINET: What's the matter with this... hic...
   bottle?
MME VIRTUEL: Water!... A drink!... Hic!... Something!
DE CHAMPRINET: (*Putting the bottle down on the dining
   table.*) Or find the corkscrew... Hic!
MME VIRTUEL: (*Suddenly.*) Oh! There. There. (*Pointing to
   the console table.*) Distilled water. There. Hic!
DE CHAMPRINET: Yes. Distilled water... Hic! (*He runs to
   the console table and quickly takes a bottle.*)
MME VIRTUEL: Be careful. Hic! Don't take the sublimate.
   Hic!
DE CHAMPRINET: (*Breaking the seal on the bottle.*) No, no,
   look. 'Distilled Water'. Hic!
   (*DE CHAMPRINET comes quickly back to the table and
   half fills MME VIRTUEL's glass. She swallows it as he pours
   some out for himself.*)
MME VIRTUEL: (*Having finished it.*) More... More... Hic!
   Another glass!
   (*They fill their glasses.*)

MME VIRTUEL: (*With a sigh of satisfaction, sitting down again.*) Ah! That does you good.

DE CHAMPRINET: (*Also drinking and beating the air with his forefinger to give more weight to what he is going to say.*) Ah! Yes.

(*MME DE CHAMPRINET bursts in from LEONIE's room.*)

MME DE C: Where's the midwife? Please. Will you come?

MME VIRTUEL: (*Raising herself from her chair.*) What's the matter?

MME DE C: I don't know. You must see for yourself. Something I can't explain.

MME VIRTUEL: (*Hurrying.*) Ah!

TOUDOUX: (*Having gone upstage right of the card table.*) What? What is it?

DE CHAMPRINET: (*Approaching.*) Something's wrong?

MME DE C: Nothing. Nothing. The midwife will...

MME VIRTUEL: (*Passing in front of MME DE CHAMPRINET who follows close behind.*) All right, I'm coming.

(*In the doorway she turns round sharply, colliding with MME DE CHAMPRINET, chest to chest.*)

Oh! Sorry.

(*To TOUDOUX.*) Make me some coffee.

TOUDOUX: What?

MME VIRTUEL: Coffee. (*As she goes out.*) Hic! Oh! They've come back again.

(*MME VIRTUEL goes out, followed by MME DE CHAMPRINET.*)

TOUDOUX: (*Annoyed, looking towards DE CHAMPRINET.*) Make me some coffee! (*To DE CHAMPRINET.*) She treats me like a servant.

DE CHAMPRINET: Ah! Good. Me too. Coffee! (*He sits in the armchair.*)

TOUDOUX: (*Taken aback.*) Oh!... Fine... Nothing else? Eh?

DE CHAMPRINET: Nothing else, thank you.

(*CLEMENCE enters and busily crosses the stage.*)

TOUDOUX: Clemence!

CLEMENCE: (*Without stopping.*) Sir?

TOUDOUX: Coffee, quickly.

CLEMENCE: (*Pushing him away, to pass.*) Oh! I've no time. (*CLEMENCE goes out right.*)

TOUDOUX: (*Taken aback.*) Oh! Oh! I apologise. (*To DE CHAMPRINET.*) I'm very sorry, she's no time. So... it will have to be later. (*He goes upstage to the dining table.*)

DE CHAMPRINET: (*Irritated, taking a cigarette out of his case.*) Charming! What a day! A dreadful dinner. My daughter's confinement. Hiccups. No coffee. (*He lights his cigarette.*)

TOUDOUX: (*Leaning back against the dining table, almost sitting on it.*) I'm terribly sorry.

DE CHAMPRINET: (*Rising and reaching the left.*) You're terribly sorry! (*He goes angrily upstage and plants himself in front of TOUDOUX with his back to the audience.*) What then?

TOUDOUX: What then what?

DE CHAMPRINET: Who's going to feed the baby?

TOUDOUX: (*Acidly.*) Its mother, not me.

DE CHAMPRINET: (*With a start.*) Its mother! You presume to make my daughter feed it?

TOUDOUX: Why not? Lots of women do.

DE CHAMPRINET: Ordinary women yes. Not in our station.

TOUDOUX: (*With a gesture, not caring.*) Oh!

DE CHAMPRINET: (*Reaching the left.*) I didn't give you my daughter to be turned into a converted soda syphon. A de Champrinet!

TOUDOUX: Sorry, a Toudoux.

DE CHAMPRINET: (*With contempt, over his shoulder.*) Yes. Oh, granted. Granted. A Toudoux. How elegant! (*Sitting left of the card table.*) Cheeseparing! To avoid paying a wet nurse or buying a bottle.

TOUDOUX: (*Shrugging his shoulders.*) Bottles make children failures.

DE CHAMPRINET: (*Rising and bowing.*) Thank you. That's how I was fed. (*He sits down again.*)

TOUDOUX: (*Floundering.*) Oh! I couldn't know.

DE CHAMPRINET: Making Léonie feed her baby!

TOUDOUX: (*His nerves on edge.*) Now listen... The child's not born yet. Do at least wait till it arrives.

DE CHAMPRINET: (*Bantering.*) Ask her to supply the milk for your coffee, while you're about it.

TOUDOUX: Oh! You're going too far.

DE CHAMPRINET: Why not?
(*MME VIRTUEL bursts in.*)

MME VIRTUEL: The maid. Where's the maid?

DE CHAMPRINET and TOUDOUX: (*Together.*) What's the matter?

MME VIRTUEL: (*Without stopping, going towards the pantry door.*) I'm asking for the maid. (*Half opening the door and calling through it.*) Adèle!

TOUDOUX: There's no point in calling Adèle. Her name's Clémence.

MME VIRTUEL: Oh! Yes, I was thinking of my last case. (*Calling.*) Clémence!

CLEMENCE: (*Off.*) Here.

TOUDOUX: She's making my father-in-law's coffee.

MME VIRTUEL: (*Passing to the centre; offhand.*) All right, he can wait.

TOUDOUX: And yours.

MME VIRTUEL: (*Changing her tone.*) Oh! Good.
(*CLEMENCE appears at the pantry door.*)

CLEMENCE: Did you call me?

MME VIRTUEL: Bring a hot water bottle to the bedroom. Quickly. (*As she finishes, she goes back quickly towards LEONIE's room.*)

CLEMENCE: Very good.
(*CLEMENCE disappears.*)

TOUDOUX: (*Catching MME VIRTUEL by the arm.*) Mme Virtuel! Mme Virtuel! (*Bringing her back to the footlights.*) I see you're busy. Has something happened?

MME VIRTUEL: Yes, something's happened. Something's certainly happened.

DE CHAMPRINET and TOUDOUX: (*Together.*) Ah?
(*DE CHAMPRINET has risen and goes to her.*)

MME VIRTUEL: No need to see any more. Now I know.
That's it.

TOUDOUX: (*Radiant.*) That's it?

DE CHAMPRINET: Already?

TOUDOUX: So you know what it is?

MME VIRTUEL: Oh, yes.

DE CHAMPRINET and TOUDOUX: (*Together.*) Ah!

TOUDOUX: (*Positively.*) It's a boy.

MME VIRTUEL: No.

DE CHAMPRINET: A girl?

MME VIRTUEL: No.

DE CHAMPRINET: Not a girl or a boy?

TOUDOUX: (*Distressed.*) Then what?

MME VIRTUEL: Nothing at all.

DE CHAMPRINET: Nothing?

TOUDOUX: What do you mean?

MME VIRTUEL: (*Waving her hand above her head to give the
impression of something flying away.*) Pht! A phantom
pregnancy.

DE CHAMPRINET: Phantom pregnancy?

TOUDOUX: (*Distressed.*) Whatever's that?

MME VIRTUEL: Something that happens. Even if you're
certain.

DE CHAMPRINET and TOUDOUX: (*Together. Overwhelmed.*)
Oh!

MME VIRTUEL: I once knew a woman who was pregnant
for twenty-five months. We were rather surprised. We
said: 'After all she's not an elephant'... Then one fine day,
pht!... Like in Lafontaine's fable.

TOUDOUX: Fable? What fable?

DE CHAMPRINET: Yes.

MME VIRTUEL: The one all midwives know. Because it's
professional. The mountain that laboured. Madame
Toudoux's been making her little mountain.

TOUDOUX: Then what? A mouse?

DE CHAMPRINET: Eh?

MME VIRTUEL: No, no. You'll have it all over again,
poor man. There's been a mistake.

TOUDOUX: (*Collapsing in the armchair.*) Mistake! There's been a mistake!

DE CHAMPRINET: (*Furious.*) A fine achievement of yours! Congratulations.

TOUDOUX: What?

DE CHAMPRINET: Can't even produce a child! When you do father something, what will it be? A rabbit?

TOUDOUX: For heavens sake! It's not my fault.

MME VIRTUEL: (*Intervening between them.*) Gentlemen! Gentlemen!

DE CHAMPRINET: (*Twirling her round and pushing her away to the left of the stage.*) Oh, go to bed, you!

MME VIRTUEL: Ohhh! He's pushed me again!
(*MME DE CHAMPRINET enters in a great state and rushes to her husband.*)

MME DE C: A phantom pregnancy! A phantom pregnancy!

TOUDOUX: Ohhh! Here she is!

DE CHAMPRINET: Yes, there's your Toudoux! That's what your Toudoux does to us!

MME DE C: Oh, if I'd known!

TOUDOUX: Now look here...

DE CHAMPRINET: I kept on telling you we should have taken a son-in-law from our world.

TOUDOUX: Ohhh! You're getting on my nerves... Your world! Your world! After all your daughter's had this pregnancy, not me. She's your world.

MME VIRTUEL: (*To TOUDOUX, who arrived next to her as he finished speaking.*) Now, now. Keep calm. Less noise.

TOUDOUX: (*To MME VIRTUEL, sending her packing.*) Shut up.

MME VIRTUEL: There's a patient. Next door!

TOUDOUX: (*To the others, passing in front of them.*) A moment ago you were attacking me because I was going to be a father. Now you are, because I'm not. Don't you know what you want? (*He has now gone back to the extreme right.*)

DE CHAMPRINET: (*Provocatively.*) What?

MME DE C: (*Passing to the left of TOUDOUX.*) Be quiet. You're absolutely ridiculous.

DE CHAMPRINET: (*Sitting, right of the card table.*) Yes, ridiculous.

TOUDOUX: All right, I'm ridiculous. I like it that way.

MME DE C: That doesn't surprise me. A man who puts chamber pots on his head!

TOUDOUX: What did you say?

MME DE C: Precisely.

TOUDOUX: (*Overcoming his feelings.*) Ohhh! I'd rather leave this house. (*He goes upstage towards the hall door.*)

MME DE C: (*Going quickly to pick up the chamber and presenting it to TOUDOUX's back, as she makes a deep curtsy, thus passing to the left of him.*) That's right... Wait, here's your hat.

TOUDOUX: (*Snatching it from her.*) My hat! (*He is about to break it, but stops when he hears De Champrinet.*)

DE CHAMPRINET: (*Quickly, still seated.*) No! No!

TOUDOUX: Eh? (*He throws it angrily onto the dining table.*)

DE CHAMPRINET: Put it on. So I can say I've seen you wearing it.

MME DE C: Yes. Yes.

TOUDOUX: What!

DE CHAMPRINET: You're the first man who's ever been seen with a chamber on his head.

TOUDOUX: Oh, am I?

DE CHAMPRINET: Yes.

TOUDOUX: Right! Now you can say you're the second. (*He picks up the chamber and crowns him with it.*)

ALL: Ohhh!

(*General uproar. They rush to DE CHAMPRINET to remove it. CLEMENCE enters with the bottle.*)

CLEMENCE: I've brought the bot... Oh!

TOUDOUX: Maybe now they'll leave me in peace!

Curtain

TAKE YOUR MEDICINE LIKE A MAN

On purge bébé

Characters

FOLLAVOINE, a porcelain manufacturer

ROSE, his maid

JULIE, his wife

TOTO, the Follavoines' son aged 7

CHOUILLOUX, a civil servant

MADAME CHOUILLOUX, his wife

TRUCHET, her cousin

*F*OLLAVOINE's study in Paris. About 1910. Downstage left is the door of FOLLAVOINE's bedroom; midstage, in a wall at an angle, the door of his wife's. In the middle of the back wall is the door into the hall, with a bookcase on each side of it: the front of each bookcase is glass or a grille, with pleated taffeta concealing the inside, two chamber pots being behind the left door of the right one, which does not open. Almost the whole of the right wall, which is straight, is taken up by a large window with net curtains covering the bottom half. Also ordinary curtains. Midstage right is a large, flat-topped desk facing the audience. On it there are files, books, a dictionary, scattered papers and a box of rubber bands. In the drawer on the actor's right is a box of sweets. Under the desk a waste paper basket. Behind the desk a chair with arms. An armchair in front of the desk at its extreme right. A sofa slightly at an angle on the left of the stage. A small, low table left of the sofa. A chair above the sofa and to its right.

NOTE: In the hall, behind the back wall, a wooden plank or something similar must be placed vertically with pieces of metal on the front, to present a hard surface for the chamber pots to break on, when they are thrown.

When the curtain rises, FOLLAVOINE is sitting on one of the arms of the desk chair, his left leg bent back on the seat, consulting a dictionary.

FOLLAVOINE: Let me see... The Urals?... Urals?... Urals?
    (A knock on the door.)
    (Angrily without raising his head.) Damn! Come in.
    (ROSE enters midstage left.)
    Well? What do you want?

ROSE: Your wife's asking for you, sir.

FOLLAVOINE: *(Diving back into the dictionary; abruptly.)* Is she? Well, let her come here. If she wants to talk to me, she knows where I am.

ROSE: *(Having come downstage centre.)* She's busy in the bath-room. She can't come.

FOLLAVOINE: Really? I can't either. I'm sorry, I'm working.

ROSE: *(Not caring.)* Very good, sir. *(She starts to go upstage.)*

FOLLAVOINE: *(Raising his head, not letting go of the diction-ary; abruptly as before.)* Anyway... What does she want?

ROSE: (*Having stopped.*) I don't know, sir.

FOLLAVOINE: Then go and ask her.

ROSE: Yes, sir. (*She goes upstage.*)

FOLLAVOINE: (*Calling her back as she is about to go out.*) By the way...

ROSE: (*Coming downstage.*) Sir?

FOLLAVOINE: I wonder... The Urals...?

ROSE: (*Not understanding.*) What?

FOLLAVOINE: The Urals? Do you know where they are?

ROSE: (*Dumbfounded.*) The Urals?

FOLLAVOINE: Yes.

ROSE: No... No... (*To clear herself.*) I haven't put them any-where. Your wife does this room.

FOLLAVOINE: (*Standing up and closing the dictionary on his forefinger to keep the place.*) You haven't put the Urals any-where!... They're mountains. Ignorant girl! Bits of land higher than the rest. Don't you know what they are?

ROSE: (*Opening her eyes wide.*) Bits of land higher than the rest?

FOLLAVOINE: Yes. What are they called?

ROSE: Molehills?

FOLLAVOINE: (*Shrugging his shoulders.*) No, not molehills. They're molehills, if they're small. If they're big, they're mountains.

ROSE: (*Dazed.*) Oh?

FOLLAVOINE: That's what the Urals are. Mountains. So they're not here in the flat.

ROSE: (*Trying to show she has understood.*) Ah, yes... They're outside.

FOLLAVOINE: (*Shrugging his shoulders.*) Of course they're outside.

ROSE: Ah! No, I haven't seen them.

FOLLAVOINE: (*Leaving the desk and pushing ROSE in a friendly way towards the door midstage left.*) Good. Thank you. That's all right.

ROSE: (*Trying to justify herself.*) You see, I haven't been in Paris long.

FOLLAVOINE: Yes... Yes, yes.

ROSE: And I don't go out much.

FOLLAVOINE: Yes, all right. Run along.

ROSE: Yes, sir.

(*ROSE goes out.*)

FOLLAVOINE: The girl doesn't know anything. What did they teach her at school? (*He comes downstage in front of the desk and leans back against it.*) She hasn't put the Urals anywhere! I believe her. (*He plunges back into the dictionary.*) Urals... Urals... (*To the Audience.*) I've found yucca, Yugoslavia, Yule and then the Zs. But no Urals, not a sign of them. If they were there, they'd be after Yule. You never find anything in this dictionary.

(*Once again he runs his eye over the column he has just read.*) (*JULIE bursts in like a whirlwind, midstage left. Slovenly appearance: a towelling bathrobe with the cord trailing along the ground behind; a little silk skirt over her nightdress which hangs down below it; curlers in her hair; stockings fallen down over old slippers. she is holding a slop pail full of water.*)

JULIE: Well, what is it? You can't come? Right?

FOLLAVOINE: (*Jumping up.*) Oh... For heaven's sake, don't always burst into the room.

JULIE: (*Apologising ironically.*) I beg your pardon. (*Tightlipped but in honeyed tones.*) You can't come? Eh?

FOLLAVOINE: (*Angrily.*) Why do I always have to come to you?

JULIE: (*With a forced smile.*) Quite right. Quite right. We're married, so...

FOLLAVOINE: What's the connection... ?

JULIE: (*As before.*) If I were someone else's wife, I probably...

FOLLAVOINE: Oh, leave me in peace. I'm busy, that's all.

JULIE: (*Putting her pail down midstage and reaching the left.*) Busy! You're busy! That's marvellous!

FOLLAVOINE: Yes, busy. (*Seeing the pail.*) Oh!

JULIE: (*Turning round.*) What?

FOLLAVOINE: Are you out of your mind? Bringing your slop pail in here now?

JULIE: Slop pail? Where's my slop pail?

FOLLAVOINE: (*Pointing to it.*) There.

JULIE: Oh, that. That's nothing. (*Very naturally.*) The water I've washed in.

FOLLAVOINE: What do you expect me to do with it?

JULIE: Nothing. I'm going to empty it.

FOLLAVOINE: Here?

JULIE: No, not here. What a silly thing to say! I don't usually empty my slop pail in your study. I have some tact.

FOLLAVOINE: Then why have you brought it to me?

JULIE: I haven't. I was just going to empty it, when Rose brought me your charming answer. So to avoid keeping you waiting...

FOLLAVOINE: Couldn't you leave it outside?

JULIE: You're getting on my nerves. If it upsets you so much, you should have come when I asked you to. But you were busy. What with? (*She strides upstage.*)

FOLLAVOINE: (*Grumbling.*) Things.

JULIE: What things?

FOLLAVOINE: (*As before.*) Things. I was looking up the Urals in the dictionary.

JULIE: The urals? You must be mad. Are you going there?

FOLLAVOINE: (*As before.*) No, I am not going there.

JULIE: (*Scornfully, as she sits on the sofa.*) Then what's it got to do with you? Why should a porcelain manufacturer care where the Urals are?

FOLLAVOINE: (*Still grumbling.*) I don't care. Baby does. The questions he asks! Children think parents know everything. (*Imitating his son.*) 'Daddy, where are the Urals? (*Grumbling, in his own voice.*) 'What?' (*His son's voice.*) Where are the Urals, Daddy?' Oh, I'd heard. I somehow had to make him say it again. (*Cursing.*) 'Where are the Urals?' How do I know? Do you?

JULIE: Yes, of course, they're... I've seen them on the map somewhere. I can't remember exactly.

FOLLAVOINE: (*Going upstage to sit at his desk and putting down the dictionary, open at the page he was reading.*) Yes,

like me. But I couldn't tell the child that. What would
he have thought? I tried to avoid the issue: 'Run along,
they're nothing to do with you. The Urals are not for
children.'

JULIE: How could you! Ridiculous!

FOLLAVOINE: Yes, I wasn't very lucky. It's a geography
question in his homework.

JULIE: (*Shrugging her shoulders.*) Obviously.

FOLLAVOINE: Why do they still teach children
geography nowadays? We've ships and railways to take
you there. And timetables that show everything.

JULIE: I don't understand.

FOLLAVOINE: If you want to know where a place is, you
don't need geography, you look in a timetable.

JULIE: Then what about the child? (*Rising and picking up her
pail.*) You won't help him?

FOLLAVOINE: What do you think? Actually I tried to
look very wise and learned. Like a man who could
answer, but prefers not to. I said: 'My boy, if I tell you,
you won't have the glory of making the effort. Try to
find it and, if you can't, then I'll tell you.'

JULIE: (*Next to him, left of the table.*) Yes, look it up.

FOLLAVOINE: I left the room very casually and, as soon
as I'd shut the door, I rushed to the dictionary, certain
I'd find them. Not a sign anywhere!

JULIE: (*Incredulous.*) In the dictionary? (*She puts down her
pail, left of the desk and moves him aside to examine the
dictionary in his place.*) Let me look...

FOLLAVOINE: (*Coming downstairs extreme right.*) Yes, do.
Really you ought to tell that governess not to stuff his
brains with things grown-ups don't know... and which
aren't even in the dictionary.

JULIE: (*Having sat down.*) Oh!... Well!

FOLLAVOINE: What?

JULIE: You've been looking under Y.

FOLLAVOINE: (*Taken aback.*) Eh?... Er... Yes.

JULIE: (*Shrugging her shoulders in pity.*) Under Y? The Urals?
I'm not surprised you couldn't find them.

FOLLAVOINE: Aren't they under Y? (*He goes round the table and moves upstage left, next to her.*)

JULIE: (*Quickly turning over the pages.*) Under Y!

FOLLAVOINE: Well, what are they under?

JULIE: (*Stopping at a page.*) You're an enormous porcelain manufacturer and you look under Y! (*Running down the column.*) Mm... 'Euphony, euphemism, eupractic...' They're under E of course. 'Eurasian, eurhythmy...' (*Taken aback.*) Good heavens!

FOLLAVOINE: What?

JULIE: They're not here!

FOLLAVOINE: (*Triumphantly, as he moves away left.*) Ah-ha! I'm not sorry. You always insist you know more than anyone else.

JULIE: (*Disconcerted.*) I don't understand. They ought to be between eupractic and Eurasian.

FOLLAVOINE: (*Angrily.*) I told you, nobody can find anything in this dictionary. It doesn't matter what letter you look it up under. All you find are words you don't want.

JULIE: (*Eyes fixed on the dictionary.*) It's very odd.

FOLLAVOINE: (*Stiffly, as he sits on the sofa.*) I can see the porcelain manufacturer's wife isn't doing any better than he is.

JULIE: (*Sharply.*) No, but I looked under E. That's more logical than Y.

FOLLAVOINE: (*Shrugging his shoulders.*) More logical than Y! Why not... U?

JULIE: (*Annoyed.*) U... U... What do you mean, U? (*A slight change of tone.*) Yes... U... Why not? Yes... Urals... Urals... I think I... Yes! (*She has pounced on the dictionary and is feverishly turning the pages.*) U... U... U...

FOLLAVOINE: (*Imitating her.*) U... U... U...

JULIE: (*Running quickly down the column.*) 'Upwind, Ur, uraemia, Urals.' (*Triumphantly.*) Yes, look. 'Urals'! Here they are.

FOLLAVOINE: (*Rushing to her.*) You've found them? (*In his hurry he doesn't see the pail and knocks his foot against it; furiously.*) Damn the thing! (*He picks up the pail and, not knowing what to do with it, puts it on the left corner of the desk. He stays there, with his forearms resting on the lid.*)

JULIE: 'Urals, a mountain chain forming the North-East boundary of Europe with Asia.'

FOLLAVOINE: (*Moving away towards the left, radiant as if he'd found them himself.*) There!

JULIE: In the singular it's also a medical preparation.

FOLLAVOINE: (*As before.*) Medical preparation! A moment ago we hadn't any Urals and now we've two different sorts. That's the history of the world. That's life.

JULIE: Yes, but which one does the child want?

FOLLAVOINE: I don't care. The mountain chain I suppose as it's geography. He can have whichever he likes. We've found them, that's the point. If there's one too many, let's forget it.

JULIE: We were looking under Y and E!

FOLLAVOINE: (*Collapsing onto the sofa.*) We might have looked all day!

JULIE: (*Rising and putting her arm through the handle of the pail.*) It was under U!

FOLLAVOINE: (*With almost unconscious impudence.*) What did I say!

JULIE: (*Dumbfounded, turning round to face him.*) What did *you* say?

FOLLAVOINE: (*Very calmly.*) Yes. Didn't I say: 'Why not U?'

JULIE: Oh, yes! You said it... You said it... Sarcastically.

FOLLAVOINE: (*Rising and going to her.*) Sarcastically? What's sarcastic about that?

JULIE: Of course it was. Laughing at me. (*Imitating him.*) 'Why not U?' (*She moves left.*)

FOLLAVOINE: No, really... you know...

JULIE: Then suddenly *I* had a sort of vision of the word.

FOLLAVOINE: (*Reaching the right, upstage of the desk.*) Vision of the word! That's marvellous. Vision of the word! How dishonest women are! I say, 'Why not U?'. Then you say, 'Yes, U, why not?'. And you call that having a sort of vision of the word! Very convenient!

JULIE: (*Furious, going to the left corner of the desk and putting her pail on it.*) This is too much. I took the dictionary. I looked it up.

FOLLAVOINE: (*Superciliously, as he comes downstage, right of the desk.*) Yes, under E.

JULIE: Under E... Under E, to start with. Like you, under Y. But then under U.

FOLLAVOINE: (*Casually, his eyes on the ceiling, as he sits in the armchair on the right in front of the desk.*) There's nothing very clever in that, after I'd said: 'Why not U?'

JULIE: (*Reaching the left.*) Yes, the way you might have said: 'Why not... P?'

FOLLAVOINE: There's no need to be rude.

JULIE: (*Turning round dumbfounded and staying for a moment nonplussed.*) What do you mean, rude?

FOLLAVOINE: I'm sorry, I'm not feeling very strong, so...

JULIE: (*Reaching the left of the desk.*) What have I done that's rude? Standing up to you? Saying what's right? (*Furiously shaking her pail on the desk.*) *I* found it. *I* found it.

FOLLAVOINE: (*Rushing to take the pail away from her.*) All right... Yes, yes... All right. All right. (*He looks round to find somewhere to put the pail.*)

JULIE: What are you looking for?

FOLLAVOINE: (*Furiously.*) I'm looking... looking... for somewhere to put this.

JULIE: Put it on the floor.

FOLLAVOINE: (*Putting it down midstage.*) Yes.

JULIE: (*Returning to the charge.*) Really, having the impudence to pretend...

FOLLAVOINE: (*Exhausted.*) Yes... All right. Agreed. You found it.

JULIE: Exactly, I did. You don't have to make concessions.

FOLLAVOINE: Please, please, that's enough. You and your Y's and E's and U's and P's! You're right. Now you'd better go and get dressed.

JULIE: (*Grumbling.*) Saying it wasn't me... ! (*She sits on the arm of the sofa.*)

FOLLAVOINE: Yes, yes... It's nearly eleven and you're still wandering about in an old dressing gown...

JULIE: (*Instinctively adjusting it.*) Go on, change the conversation.

FOLLAVOINE: ... with your hair in curlers and your
stockings hanging down over your heels!

JULIE: (*Abruptly pulling up her stockings.*) Whose heels do
you expect them to hang down over? Yours?

FOLLAVOINE: Nobody's.

JULIE: There. I've pulled them up.

FOLLAVOINE: That won't stop them falling down again.
Can't you attach them to something?

JULIE: I've no suspenders on.

FOLLAVOINE: Then put them on.

JULIE: They'd be no use. I've no corset.

FOLLAVOINE: (*Reaching the right, near the armchair in front
of the desk.*) Then put a corset on, dammit!

JULIE: Dammit yourself! Say right out you expect me to
wear a ballgown to do the bathroom. (*She has picked up
the pail by putting her arm through the handle and goes upstage
towards her room.*)

FOLLAVOINE: For heaven's sake! Who's asked you to do
the bathroom? Anyone would think you'd no servant.
Where's the maid?
(*JULIE had reached the doorway and, turning round as if cut
to the quick, prowls downstage to him. She then gets rid of the
pail by putting it on the floor at his feet.*)

JULIE: (*Arms crossed, straight into his face.*) Have my bathroom done by the maid?

FOLLAVOINE: (*To escape a new argument, passing in front of
her and reaching the left.*) Oh...

JULIE: (*Not giving in and keeping in step, parallel to him and
upstage.*) Thanks very much. So everything gets chipped
or broken! No, no. I do that myself.
(*She leaves him and, reaching the extreme right, goes and sits in
the armchair in front of the desk.*)

FOLLAVOINE: There's no point in having a maid if she's
useless.

JULIE: (*Stretching out her right leg, half bare, on the pail, like a
stool.*) She's not useless. She's there.

FOLLAVOINE: Then what's she up to, while you're doing
her work?

JULIE: (*Slightly taken aback.*) Well, she... she watches me.

FOLLAVOINE: She watches you! I pay a girl four hundred francs a month to watch you!

JULIE: Don't always talk about what you have to pay. It's vulgar.

FOLLAVOINE: I don't care how vulgar it it. When I pay a woman four hundred francs a month, I think...

JULIE: (*Rising, without troubling to withdraw her leg from the pail but simply letting it slide over the top onto the floor and going to him.*) Now look. I haven't asked to be paid, have I? So long as it doesn't cost you any more, why should you care if she does the work or me?

FOLLAVOINE: I care... I care... because I've a maid to do my wife's work, not a wife to do the maid's. Or if I have, I'll get rid of the maid.

JULIE: (*With big indignant gestures.*) So that's it. We were bound to come to this. You're trading me for a servant. (*She reaches the extreme right.*)

FOLLAVOINE: (*Copying her, reaching the extreme left.*) I'm trading her for a servant now!

JULIE: (*Turning round to face him.*) Yes, you are.

FOLLAVOINE: (*Having run out of arguments.*) Look, pull up your stockings. You'd better.

JULIE: (*Sharply pulling up her stockings.*) Yes, oh... (*Resuming.*) All this because I like to do the bathroom myself! (*Going upstage extreme right beyond the desk.*) You must be the first husband who's ever objected to his wife doing the housework.

FOLLAVOINE: Between doing the housework and...

JULIE: (*Angrily, as she automatically tidies the papers on his desk.*) You'd rather I behaved like other women?... Do nothing but buy clothes and spend a fortune?

FOLLAVOINE: (*Seeing what she is doing and anxious about his papers.*) Oh!... Oh! (*He rushes to defend them.*)

JULIE: (*As before.*) Never at home. Driving, racing, shopping...

FOLLAVOINE: (*Protecting his papers as best he can.*) No, please... please.

JULIE: (*Continuing as before.*) ... Skating all morning. Skating all afternoon.

FOLLAVOINE: (*As before.*) Please. Stop it.

JULIE: (*As before.*) What a life!

FOLLAVOINE: (*As before.*) No, that doesn't go there. Leave them alone. (*He makes her move away to the right.*)

JULIE: What is it?

FOLLAVOINE: (*Trying to put his papers in order.*) My papers, for heaven's sake! I never asked you to tidy them up.

JULIE: I can't bear the sight of an untidy desk.

FOLLAVOINE: Then don't look at it. Leave it alone.

JULIE: (*Coming downstage right.*) I don't care a fig for your desk. (*She picks up her pail in passing.*)

FOLLAVOINE: Then show you don't. Go and tidy up your own room. (*Grumbling between his teeth.*) This passion for cleaning up everywhere! (*He is seated at the desk.*)

JULIE: (*Returning to the charge, having gone round the desk to the left corner.*) So that's how you want me to be!

FOLLAVOINE: (*Losing his temper and almost shouting.*) Want you to be! Want you to be! What are you talking about?

JULIE: Like other women?

FOLLAVOINE: (*Exasperated, as he tidies his papers.*) How do I know? Just don't mess about with my papers. That's not asking much.

JULIE: (*Not giving in, going to the extreme left with the gait and gestures of a minuet, making the pail swing like a censer and threatening the carpet.*) A leader of Society perhaps? (*Changing her tone.*) I'm sorry, that's not how I was brought up.

FOLLAVOINE: (*Having had more than enough.*) Yes, good. That's splendid.

JULIE: (*Coming back towards him at the left corner of the desk and putting her pail down on his papers as he is about to pick them up.*) You know my family had...

FOLLAVOINE: (*Prevented by the pail from picking up his papers.*) Yes... Now, look...

JULIE: (*Picking up the pail.*) ... my family had...

FOLLAVOINE: (*Raising his eyes to heaven.*) Ohhh!

JULIE: ... only one thing in mind, as far as my education was concerned. To make me a good housewife.

FOLLAVOINE: Now listen. This is all very interesting, but it's eleven o'clock and...

JULIE: (*Cutting him short.*) I don't care... I was taught to do everything myself... Not rely on other people... Because you never know if you'll always have other people to serve you. (*With dignity she reaches the left.*)

FOLLAVOINE: (*Shrugging his shoulders and raising his eyes to heaven.*) Your stockings!

JULIE: Oh, damn! (*Without troubling to sit down, she quickly pulls up her stockings, one after the other, and resumes.*) I was trained like that as a child. So it's become second nature. (*Sitting in the armchair, right of the desk.*) Now is that a good thing? Or a bad? (*Putting her elbows on the edge of the desk, her head on her hand.*) All I can say is: I get it from my mother.

FOLLAVOINE: (*With no ulterior motive, busy looking through his papers.*) Oh!... My mother-in-law.

JULIE: (*Stiffly, with her head half turned towards him.*) No... My mother.

FOLLAVOINE: (*As before.*) Yes. It's the same thing.

JULIE: (*As before.*) Possibly. But 'my mother' is tender, affectionate, polite. 'My mother-in-law' implies something unfeeling, bitter-sweet, discourteous, that's quite unjustified.

FOLLAVOINE: (*As before.*) Yes, all right.

JULIE: I said 'my mother'. She is my mother. There's no point in correcting me and saying 'my mother-in-law'.

FOLLAVOINE: I only said 'my mother-in-law', because as far as I'm concerned...

JULIE: (*Standing straight up as if moved by a spring, back to the audience, hands clenched on the edge of the desk and body leaning forward as if to devour him.*) Hasn't she always been perfectly correct? Are you objecting to something?

FOLLAVOINE: (*Forcefully, thrusting his body as far as possible into the back of the chair to get her out of reach.*) No, no. What are you trying to make out? It's simply that as far as I'm concerned, your mother...

JULIE: (*Haughtily and peremptorily, reaching centre stage and turning round.*) Please. That's quite enough about my mother.

FOLLAVOINE: (*Dumbfounded.*) What?

JULIE: It's a fact. You're always picking on the poor woman. Making nasty remarks on the slightest excuse.

FOLLAVOINE: Me!

JULIE: Simply because I brought my slop pail into your study.

FOLLAVOINE: Really, this is too....

JULIE: (*Sliding her arm under the handle of the pail which is still on the desk.*) I'll take the pail away. There. Look. It's nothing to make a fuss about.

FOLLAVOINE: (*Grumbling, as he pretends to bury himself in his papers.*) All right. It doesn't matter.

JULIE: (*Muttering, as she goes upstage to the door of her room.*) Carrying on like this about a wretched slop pail! As if I'd committed a crime! (*Having reached the doorway she stops. A thought crosses her mind. She turns sharply round, comes downstage to the desk and puts her pail on it in the same place; as before.*) Another time when you want to complain about something...

FOLLAVOINE: (*Interrupting her.*) No, please... please.

JULIE: (*Taken aback.*) What?

FOLLAVOINE: Here's the pail again!

JULIE: (*Between her teeth.*) Idiot! (*Resuming.*) When you want to complain about something, you might tell me straight out... not start attacking mother. (*She trips lightly downstage, leaving the pail on the desk.*)

FOLLAVOINE: (*Losing his temper and going to her.*) For God's sake! What have I said?

JULIE: Nothing, nothing. As a last resort of course you have to play the hypocrite.

FOLLAVOINE: (*Exhausted and powerless to struggle.*) Ohhh! (*He goes upstage left.*)

JULIE: (*Having gone upstage of the desk, automatically starting to tidy it.*) I always know what you mean... when you don't say anything.

FOLLAVOINE: (*Turning round.*) This is the limit. I say...
(*Rushing at her as he sees her rummaging among his papers.*)
No, no, no! Will you leave my papers alone! (*He takes
her place, making her go left of the desk.*) Why do you have
this passion for..?

JULIE: (*Peremptorily.*) I like tidiness.

FOLLAVOINE: (*Shrugging his shoulders.*) You like tidiness!
You like tidiness! (*Pointing to the pail and holding it out to
her.*) Look at this.

JULIE: (*Taking it.*) Well?

FOLLAVOINE: (*Grumbling.*) You like tidiness! It wouldn't
be a bad idea to do something about your dress. (*Rising.*)
A moment ago you started to do the right thing. You
almost took your pail away. But you brought it back
again...

JULIE: (*Peremptorily, cutting him short.*) I had to talk to you.

FOLLAVOINE: (*Pushing her gently towards the door of her
room.*) Yes, all right. Later.

JULIE: No, not later. You can imagine, I only asked you
just now to...

FOLLAVOINE: (*Near to the sofa, as is she.*) Please. It's
eleven o'clock and you still haven't begun to get
dressed. The Chouilloux's are coming to lunch and...

JULIE: Chouilloux's! Chouilloux's! I don't give a damn for
the Chouilloux's.

FOLLAVOINE: No, but I do. Chouilloux is a man it's
most important for me to be nice to...

JULIE: Possibly, but I'm sorry he'll have to wait. Because
of Baby. And between Baby and Chouilloux I think the
choice is clear.

FOLLAVOINE: (*Losing his temper.*) Ohhh! What about
Baby!

JULIE: (*Passing in front of him and reaching the right.*) Or go
on, say that Chouilloux is more important. (*She sits in the
armchair in front of the desk, with the pail on her knees.*)

FOLLAVOINE: (*Almost shouting.*) No, no. That has nothing
to do with it. I'm not comparing Baby with Chouilloux.
But if you're entertaining an important visitor, you put
yourself out for him. That doesn't mean he's more

important than the family. Chouilloux is arriving early to discuss an important deal...

JULIE: Discuss it then. What's it got to do with me?

FOLLAVOINE: He'll be here any moment. You can't receive him in a dirty dressing gown, with your hair in curlers, your slop pail on your knees and your stockings falling over your heels.

JULIE: (*Angrily putting the pail down in front of her.*) My stockings! You're driving me mad! (*Standing with one foot on the pail and bending down to pull up her stockings.*) What about them? Doesn't your friend Chouilloux know what happens to stockings when you've no suspenders on? Eh? When his wife gets up, does she wear a ball gown? (*She angrily pulls up her stockings.*)

FOLLAVOINE: I don't know what his wife wears when she gets up. I'm simply telling you you're not properly dressed for people who are coming to lunch for the first time. (*He goes upstage.*)

JULIE: (*Rummaging among the things on his desk, looking for something.*) You're in a morning coat. That makes up for it.

FOLLAVOINE: (*Turning round.*) I am properly dressed. (*Seeing what she is doing.*) *What* are you looking for? *What* are you looking for?

JULIE: (*Picking up a box of rubber bands.*) Your elastic bands.

FOLLAVOINE: (*Upstage of the desk.*) Why? What for?

JULIE: (*Putting the box back on the desk and sitting down again.*) To stop you carrying on about my stockings. (*She puts an elastic band round each leg.*)

FOLLAVOINE: They're rubber bands for my papers. Not garters.

JULIE: (*Finishing putting them on.*) They're not garters, because they're not used for garters. But when I do use them for garters, they become garters.

FOLLAVOINE: (*Discouraged, reaching the right.*) Ohhh! Your untidiness...

JULIE: (*Shrugging her shoulders.*) You're properly dressed! It's ridiculous! Wearing a morning coat at eleven in the morning! For Monsieur Chouilloux!... That cuckold!

FOLLAVOINE: (*Looking at her, astonished.*) Cuckold? What do you mean? What do you know about it?

JULIE: (*Happy to put him in the wrong.*) You told me.

FOLLAVOINE: Me!

JULIE: I can't have dreamt it, can I? I don't know the man. He's not a friend of mine. I've no reason to run him down. (*She passes in front of him and reaches the left.*)

FOLLAVOINE: (*Leaning back on the corner of the desk.*) Chouilloux, a cuckold! You can't say that!

JULIE: (*Coming downstage towards him.*) Apparently you can. You did.

FOLLAVOINE: I did... I did... when I didn't need him. But now I do...

JULIE: (*Nose to nose.*) He's not a cuckold any more?

FOLLAVOINE: No... Yes... It's no business of ours. We're not entertaining him in that capacity. (*He reaches the extreme right.*)

JULIE: Obviously.

FOLLAVOINE: (*Going upstage beyond the desk on the extreme right.*) At the moment he's a man who can be extremely useful to me.

JULIE: How?

FOLLAVOINE: For a big scheme I'm planning. It would take too long to explain.

JULIE: (*Reaching the right.*) Yes, you've always big ideas when money's involved.

FOLLAVOINE: Does it upset you him being a cuckold?

JULIE: No, no. I don't care how many times he is. What does upset me is you saddling me with his wife for lunch.

FOLLAVOINE: (*Left of the desk.*) I can't ask him without her. It isn't done.

JULIE: Oh? And her lover, her cousin Monsieur Horace Truchet? You had to ask her lover too?

FOLLAVOINE: Yes, I did. It's customary. They're invited everywhere together. It would have been tactless not to ask him. Chouilloux might have wondered what it meant. It isn't done.

JULIE: (*Leaning back on the desk, her arms crossed.*)
Marvellous! So now we've all three of them. Full scale
adultery! So moral! (*Picking up her pail and reaching the
left.*) Charming guests for your wife! And a fine example
for Toto!

FOLLAVOINE: (*Coming downstage.*) Toto!... He's seven!

JULIE: He won't always be.

FOLLAVOINE: No. But in the meantime he is.

JULIE: I see. I see. It's the same with his moral health as
his physical. You don't care.

FOLLAVOINE: (*Raising his arms to heaven as he goes upstage
of the desk.*) What does that mean? What are you imply-
ing now?

JULIE: (*Promptly putting her pail down midstage and
immediately going upstage to her husband who is now seated
at the desk.*) It's obvious. For the last hour I've been
trying to talk to you about Baby to discuss his health
and I can't get a word in. Whenever I open my mouth
and say 'Baby', you say 'Chouilloux'. Nothing but
Chouilloux. Chouilloux, Chouilloux, Chouilloux all
the time.

FOLLAVOINE: (*His patience nearly exhausted.*) What is it?
What's the matter? What do you want to tell me?

JULIE: (*Peremptorily.*) I've got to talk to you.

FOLLAVOINE: Talk then.

JULIE: Oh?... About time. (*She comes downstage and sits on
her pail as if it were a stool.*)

FOLLAVOINE: (*Leaping from his chair and pounding the
desk.*) No! No!

JULIE: (*Dumbfounded.*) What?

FOLLAVOINE: Can't you find any other seat? Do you
think a slop pail's made to sit on?

JULIE: It doesn't matter. I'm all right.

FOLLAVOINE: It's nothing to do with your being
all right. A slop pail's not a seat. Do please sit on
a chair.

JULIE: (*Looking him up and down, then turning her head away
scornfully, as she rises.*) You're so grand.

FOLLAVOINE: I'm not being grand. You could easily upset it. I don't want your dirty water all over my carpet.

JULIE: There'd be no harm done. It would wash it.

FOLLAVOINE: Thank you. How kind! I'd prefer something else. Anyhow, what about Baby! What's the matter with him?

JULIE: (*Scornfully, submitting.*) Oh?... I may?

FOLLAVOINE: (*His nerves on edge.*) Yes, you may.

JULIE: (*Having gone to get the chair next to the sofa, bringing it near the desk next to him and sitting on it.*) Well... I'm very upset.

FOLLAVOINE: Oh!

JULIE: I'm not pleased with Toto.

FOLLAVOINE: Yes... What's he done?

JULIE: He hasn't been this morning.

FOLLAVOINE: (*Repeating like an echo, not understanding.*) He hasn't been?

JULIE: No.

FOLLAVOINE: He hasn't been... where?

JULIE: (*Suddenly flaring up.*) Nowhere. He hasn't been. That's all.

FOLLAVOINE: (*Understanding.*) Ah! Yes, to the...

JULIE: (*Brutally.*) Exactly. Yes. (*Changing her tone.*) We've tried... four times. Without result... Once, yes... Oh... Nothing. (*Holding up her little finger with her thumbnail against the last joint.*) As big as that.

FOLLAVOINE: Oh!

JULIE: (*Raising her eyes to heaven.*) And hard.

FOLLAVOINE: (*Nodding.*) Yes... He's constipated.

JULIE: (*Annoyed.*) He's constipated.

FOLLAVOINE: Yes... Well?... What do you want me to do?

JULIE: (*Scandalized.*) What do *I* want?

FOLLAVOINE: Dammit, I can't go for him!

JULIE: (*Rising.*) What a mean thing to say! Of course you can't go for him.

FOLLAVOINE: Well?

JULIE: A lot of good your going for him would do! But because you can't go for people, that's no reason to let

them die. (*Coming downstage left.*) Really, you're so
heartless!

FOLLAVOINE: (*Rising and going to her; good-natured.*) Now
you don't want me to burst into tears because the child's
a little constipated.

JULIE: Why not? You must never treat constipation lightly.

FOLLAVOINE: (*Incredulous.*) Oh?

JULIE: (*Importantly.*) I once read that a bastard son of Louis
XV nearly died of persistent constipation at the age of
seven.

FOLLAVOINE: Perhaps. But it was persistent and he was
a bastard, neither of which applies to Toto.

JULIE: Yes, but Toto's seven like him. And constipated
like him.

FOLLAVOINE: Well, you only have to give him a laxative.

JULIE: (*Pityingly.*) Oh... Naturally.

FOLLAVOINE: Then go on, do it. (*He reaches the right.*)

JULIE: Thank you. I'm not asking your permission. I'm
asking what to give him.

FOLLAVOINE: (*Having come back to her.*) Castor oil. He
takes it easily and it always works.

JULIE: (*With an instinctive horror.*) Castor oil! No, no! I can't
stand it. I bring it up at once.

FOLLAVOINE: You're not going to take it, he is.

JULIE: Yes, but it's the same thing. The mere sight of it!
Or mention of it!... (*She shudders.*) Oh, no!... Anyway I
can't think why you're making all these complications.
We've a bottle of Hunyadi-Janos in the medicine
cupboard, I don't see why we shouldn't use that,
because you prefer castor oil.

FOLLAVOINE: (*Dumbfounded.*) Me!

JULIE: (*unanswerably.*) We have Hunyadi-Janos. Baby will
take Hunyadi-Janos.

FOLLAVOINE: (*Reaching the extreme right.*) Then give him
Hunyadi-Janos... But I don't see why you had to come
and consult me. (*He goes upstage extreme right to his desk.*)

JULIE: To find out what I had to do.

FOLLAVOINE: Oh? Good. I hadn't realized. (*He sits at
the desk.*)

JULIE: It's dreadful, having to dose the poor child. It's always the same. Every time his grandmother takes him out...

FOLLAVOINE: (*Absent-mindedly, as he looks at a letter.*) Which grandmother?

JULIE: (*Curtly.*) His grandmother! He hasn't got three dozen. Your mother's in Düsseldorf, so it must be mine. (*She sits on the sofa.*)

FOLLAVOINE: Ah, yes. Yes... Your mother.

JULIE: Yes, of course, my mother. (*Imitating him.*) *Your* mother! *Your* mother! I know she's my mother. The way you say '*Your* mother'! It always sounds as though you're sneering at her.

FOLLAVOINE: (*Dumbfounded.*) Me!

JULIE: (*Reverting to her theme.*) It's always like this. Every time she takes him out. She stuffs him full of cakes and sweets...

FOLLAVOINE: (*Writing.*) Oh, well... All grandmothers are like that.

JULIE: Perhaps. But she was wrong. Especially as I asked her not to.

FOLLAVOINE: The poor woman didn't think...

JULIE: (*Getting angry.*) Didn't think, didn't think! I know. But she was still wrong.

FOLLAVOINE: (*Indulgent.*) Oh, well...

JULIE: (*Getting carried away.*) There's no 'Oh well' about it. It's extraordinary the way you always side with mother. I tell you she was wrong. Well, she was wrong.

FOLLAVOINE: (*For the sake of peace.*) Good... Good.

JULIE: So now the child won't go and we have to dose him.

FOLLAVOINE: Yes, it's annoying. But it won't kill him.

JULIE: (*Drawing herself up, shocked.*) So I should hope. Won't kill him! (*Pouncing on him and shaking him.*) What a monstrous thing to say about your own son! 'It won't kill him'! He's your child, you know. Don't start looking as though he might not be. He's yours.

FOLLAVOINE: So I should hope.

JULIE: I'm not like Chouilloux's wife. I don't get my cousins to do your work for you.

FOLLAVOINE: All right. Leave me in peace.

JULIE: (*Coming back downstage and reaching the right.*) When I have a child, he's my husband's.

FOLLAVOINE: Who said he wasn't?

JULIE: (*Sitting in the armchair in front of the desk.*) You don't behave like a father at all. It would serve you right if he wasn't your son.

FOLLAVOINE: (*Shrugging his shoulders.*) You're being silly.

JULIE: It would serve you right if he was a bastard... And his father was... (*Not finding a name.*) Louis XV.

FOLLAVOINE: (*With a chuckle.*) Louis XV!

JULIE: Yes.

FOLLAVOINE: That would make history!

JULIE: Laugh away. Go on, laugh away.

FOLLAVOINE: (*Fed up.*) Now listen to me. That's enough. The subject's closed. We've decided to dose the child. So go on, do it.

JULIE: (*Her head lowered, looking into space; worried.*) There'll be a scene.

FOLLAVOINE: (*Rising.*) All right, there'll be a scene. That's too bad. Now please go away. Before Chouilloux arrives, I've got to collect my thoughts and plan my approach. Run along... go and get dressed. (*He goes upstage towards the bookcase nearest to him.*)

JULIE: (*Rising with an effort and going upstage towards her room, mumbling broken sentences in a distressed voice.*) Poor child... when I think of having to dose him... It makes me ill...

FOLLAVOINE: (*Having opened the right hand door of the bookcase, turning round and seeing the pail still in the middle of the stage; calling.*) Julie! Julie!

JULIE: (*In the same doleful voice.*) What?

FOLLAVOINE: (*Pointing to the pail.*) Please! Your pail! I really have seen enough of it.

JULIE: (*Furiously, coming downstage to get her pail.*) My pail! My pail! It's always my pail! Chouilloux, my pail! My pail, Chouilloux! That's all I ever hear!

FOLLAVOINE: For heaven's sake! A study's no place for slop pails. (*Having taken a chamber pot out of the bookcase, he displays it as he finishes speaking.*)

JULIE: (*Immediately growing calm; teasing him.*) What impudence! You make a fuss about my slop pail and now you're parading around with a chamber pot!

FOLLAVOINE: (*Annoyed.*) A chamber pot!

JULIE: Unless you're launching a new sort of headdress.

FOLLAVOINE: A chamber pot! You dare to compare your slop pail... with this! Your slop pail is only... your slop pail. In other words a nasty, mean object, to be hidden not displayed. (*Admiringly, as if it were a work of art, holding it out at his fingertips.*) But this is...

JULIE: (*Cutting him short, coming downstage towards the right.*) This is... a chamber pot. In other words a nasty, mean object, to be hidden, not displayed.

FOLLAVOINE: (*Coming downstage towards her; lyrically.*) Yes, for you, for the profane. But for me it's something nobler, grander... which I don't blush to display here. It's the product of my factory. A sample of my industry. My stock in trade. My daily bread.

JULIE: (*With a little ironical curtsy.*) Eat it up then. (*She reaches the right.*)

FOLLAVOINE: (*Having gone and put the chamber on the small table left of the sofa.*) Laugh away. But you won't always laugh. When it gives us an income of three hundred thousand pounds...

JULIE: (*Leaning back against the right-hand table and passing the pail from her tired right arm to her left.*) Three hundred thousand pounds a year from chamber pots?

FOLLAVOINE: (*Going to her.*) From chamber pots, exactly. That surprises you. But if God wills... and Chouilloux does too, it will happen.

JULIE: What's all this nonsense?

FOLLAVOINE: It's not nonsense. I didn't tell you, to make it a surprise if it came off. But as it is... Well, you don't know, but the Government's chief concern at the moment is to improve life for the Army. They're looked after, mollycoddled, wrapped up in cotton wool. Now they're being issued with bedroom slippers.

JULIE: Bedroom slippers for the Army?

FOLLAVOINE: Yes.

JULIE: How very martial!

FOLLAVOINE: Of course it's not stopping there. Now they've decided men mustn't risk catching cold by getting up in the middle of the night and going out of doors in the wind and the rain. So in future every man in the French army will have his own chamber pot.

JULIE: (*Astounded.*) No!

FOLLAVOINE: With his name and number on it.

JULIE: (*Open mouthed.*) That's the limit!

FOLLAVOINE: The result is they've asked for tenders for this new... military equipment and as a porcelain manufacturer I've decided to quote. Chouilloux is coming here like a Deus ex Machina...

JULIE: What does that mean?

FOLLAVOINE: (*Taken aback.*) What?

JULIE: A day sex machina?

FOLLAVOINE: (*With an indulgent smile.*) Day sex machina! Deus ex machina.

JULIE: (*Sharply.*) That's what I said. I'm asking what it means.

FOLLAVOINE: What it... ?

JULIE: Yes.

FOLLAVOINE: Well... er...

JULIE: Go on.

FOLLAVOINE: It's not easy to say.

JULIE: Why? Is it rude?

FOLLAVOINE: (*Laughing.*) No, it isn't rude. Deus ex machina is... is just an expression. The Greeks... The Greeks used it to mean... the big white chief. The great Panjandrum.

JULIE: A fat man.

FOLLAVOINE: No, no. A man with great influence.

JULIE: Oh!... A figure of speech,

FOLLAVOINE: A figure of speech. Well, that's what Chouilloux is. He's chairman of the committee that's deciding which type they're going to use. Now do you understand why we have to be nice to him? I've a patent for unbreakable china, haven't I? So if Chouilloux persuades the committee to use unbreakable china, that's that. My fortune's made.

JULIE: (*After thinking for a moment, nodding her head.*) Yes...
And what will that lead to?

FOLLAVOINE: (*Getting carried away.*) A gold mine. I'll be
sole supplier to the French army.

JULIE: Supplier of chamber pots to the French army?

FOLLAVOINE: (*Proudly.*) Every pot in the army.

JULIE: (*Frowning.*) Everyone will know?

FOLLAVOINE: (*As before.*) Of course they'll know.

JULIE: Oh, no!... No, no, no, no, no, no! I will not be the
wife of a man who sells chamber pots.

FOLLAVOINE: What a ridiculous idea! It will make our
fortune.

JULIE: I don't care. It's disgusting.

FOLLAVOINE: For heaven's sake! What else am I doing
now? I sell chamber pots. I sell them every day. Not on
that scale. But I sell them.

JULIE: (*Going back in front of the desk.*) You sell them,
you sell them... the way you sell other things. You're
a porcelain manufacturer, so of course you sell what
you produce. That's normal, that's fine. But to start
specialising and be the man who sells nothing but
chamber pots! No, no, not even for the State, no!

FOLLAVOINE: (*Taken aback; panic-stricken.*) You're out of
your mind. Do think.

JULIE: (*Leaning back on the desk with her arms crossed.*)
I have thought. You're very kind. But I don't want to go
through life with a chamber pot as a halo. I don't want
to be pointed at in every drawing room as the wife of
the chamber pot man. No, no.

FOLLAVOINE: (*More and more panic stricken at the thought of
his whole edifice collapsing.*) Oh, if I'd ever thought... Oh...
Please... Don't say that to Chouilloux.

JULIE: (*Scornfully.*) I have nothing to say to Chouilloux.

FOLLAVOINE: Listen. I'll see... Perhaps there's some way
to arrange things, to... to use a front man, I don't know.
But don't ruin everything, please. When Chouilloux
arrives, be nice. be polite.

JULIE: I'm not usually impolite. I know how to behave.

(*She goes nearer to him.*)

FOLLAVOINE: Of course you do, I...

JULIE: My father entertained Monsieur Thiers.

FOLLAVOINE: Yes. Oh... you can't have been born.

JULIE: Possibly, but my father entertained him all the
  same. (*She passes in front of him.*)

FOLLAVOINE: Did he? Good. That's fine then. Now...
  (*Pushing her gently towards the door of her room.*) Go and
  give Baby his medicine. Get dressed and take away
  your slop pail, eh? Please.

JULIE: (*Going with him towards her bedroom door.*) All right.
  I've got it. There's no need for you to keep on telling
  me what I have to do.
  (*The bell rings.*)

FOLLAVOINE: There's the bell. It must be Chouilloux.
  Please, do hurry. If he came in now...

JULIE: (*In the doorway.*) Well? He'd see me.

FOLLAVOINE: (*Making her go out.*) Exactly. And like this,
  I'd rather he didn't.
  (*JULIE goes out.*)
  (*Closing the door and coming downstage extreme left.*) Oh,
  women! Women! They do make life complicated. (*In
  passing, he picks up the chamber.*) Where is Chouilloux,
  what are they waiting for?
  (*He goes to the hall door, half opens it and chances a peep. Then
  he opens it fully.*)
  No one there?... (*Calling into the wings.*) Rose!... Rose! (*He
  comes downstage, without closing the door and goes to
  his desk.*)
  (*ROSE enters.*)

ROSE: (*In the doorway.*) Sir?

FOLLAVOINE: (*Standing at the desk with the chamber in his
  left hand.*) What is it? Who rang?

ROSE: A lady, wanting you to pull a tooth out.

FOLLAVOINE: What's that to do with me? You should
  have sent her to the dentist.

ROSE: I did. She went upstairs.

FOLLAVOINE: (*Passing the chamber from his left hand to his
  right.*) Damnation! It keeps on happening!

ROSE: (*From now on keeping her eyes fixed on the chamber.*) Oh!... Sir, do you know?

FOLLAVOINE: What?

ROSE: You're holding your pottie.

FOLLAVOINE: Yes, I do know. Thank you.

ROSE: Ah!... I thought you'd forgotten... Sorry.

FOLLAVOINE: Anyway it's not a pottie. It's an item of military equipment. (*He puts it down on his right on the papers that are on the left of the desk.*)

ROSE: Oh?... Funny, it looks like a pottie.

FOLLAVOINE: (*Dismissing her.*) Yes. All right... Be off with you.

(*ROSE goes out into the hall.*)

(*Sitting at the desk and calculating.*) Let's see... On a peace-time footing... the French army has about three hundred thousand men... at one pot a man, if the pot costs...

(*JULIE, dressed* as before, *thrusts the top half of her body through the half open door of her room.*)

JULIE: Bastien! Come a moment.

FOLLAVOINE: (*Still engrossed in his problem; curtly, without raising his head.*) Sh! I've no time.

JULIE: (*Coming downstage with the pail in her right hand.*) I tell you to come. He won't take his medicine.

FOLLAVOINE: (*As before, raising his head.*) Make him. Use your authority. (*Seeing the pail on her arm.*) Ohhh!

JULIE: What?

FOLLAVOINE: (*Indignantly, drawing himself up.*) You've brought your slop pail back again.

JULIE: I've had no time to empty it. Please come. I...

FOLLAVOINE: (*Erupting.*) No, no. I've seen enough of that thing. Take it away. Take it away.

JULIE: Yes. All right... Please. Baby is...

FOLLAVOINE: Go on, go on. Take it away.

JULIE: I keep telling you...

FOLLAVOINE: I don't give a damn. Take it away.

JULIE: (*Fed up, coming downstage and putting the pail down in the middle of the stage.*) You're getting on my nerves.

FOLLAVOINE: (*Dumbfounded.*) What?

JULIE: (*In front of the sofa.*) 'Take it away. Take it away.'! I'm not your servant.

FOLLAVOINE: (*Not believing his ears.*) What did you say?

JULIE: It's a fact. I always have to do everything in this house. My pail annoys you? Then take it away yourself.

FOLLAVOINE: Me!

JULIE: I brought it in, it's your turn to take it out.

FOLLAVOINE: (*Coming downstage towards her.*) For God's sake! It's your washing water, not mine.

JULIE: (*Passing in front of him.*) Yes?... Well, I give it to you. Now you needn't have any scruples. (*She avoids him by going upstage centre towards her room.*)

FOLLAVOINE: (*Running after her and trying to catch her by the hem of her dressing gown.*) Julie!... Julie, be sensible.

JULIE: I've given it to you. It's yours.
(*JULIE goes out into her room.*)

FOLLAVOINE: (*In the doorway, speaking through the half open door.*) Julie! Will you take it away!... Julie!
(*ROSE enters from the hall, followed by CHOUILLOUX. He is wearing a morning coat, with the rosette of the Legion of Honour in his buttonhole.*)

ROSE: (*Announcing.*) Monsieur Chouilloux.

FOLLAVOINE: Will you take...!

CHOUILLOUX: (*Coming downstage.*) Good morning, dear Monsieur Follavoine.

FOLLAVOINE: (*Without turning round.*) Ohhh! Go to hell!
(*ROSE goes out.*)
(*Turning round and seeing CHOUILLOUX.*) I am sorry... Monsieur Chouilloux! Already!

CHOUILLOUX: Am I too early?

FOLLAVOINE: Not at all. Not at all. I was talking to my wife. So I didn't hear the bell.

CHOUILLOUX: I rang it though. And the door was opened. (*Playfully.*) I haven't yet acquired the gift of walking through walls.

FOLLAVOINE: (*Flattering.*) How witty! How witty!

CHOUILLOUX: (*Modestly.*) Well...

FOLLAVOINE: (*Taking his hat.*) Can I relieve you of this?

CHOUILLOUX: Too kind! (*Coming downstage and stopping with amazement at the sight of the pail.*) Well!

FOLLAVOINE: (*Having put the hat on the shelf of the lefthand bookcase, coming quickly downstage to stand between CHOUILLOUX and the pail.*) I'm sorry. Forgive me, my wife came in a moment ago. She was holding it and absent-mindedly she... (*Having gone upstage to the hall door, he opens it and calls.*) Rose!... Rose!

ROSE: (*Off.*) Sir?

FOLLAVOINE: Come along, then. (*He comes downstage to CHOUILLOUX, so that the pail is standing between them.*) Really, I'm so embarrassed. Especially the day I'm honoured...

CHOUILLOUX: (*Bowing repeatedly.*) Please. Please.

FOLLAVOINE: (*Continually bowing.*) I say what I think, Monsieur Chouilloux. I say what I think.

CHOUILLOUX: (*As before.*) Too kind... Yes, really...
(*ROSE appears at the hall door.*)

ROSE: You called, sir?

FOLLAVOINE: Yes. Take this pail away.

ROSE: (*Amazed.*) Oh!... What's it doing there?

FOLLAVOINE: My wife left it... by mistake.

ROSE: She must have been searching for it everywhere. (*She picks it up.*)

FOLLAVOINE: Yes, that's right, run along. (*He goes upstage behind ROSE, pushing her towards the door of JULIE's room.*) Tell my wife Monsieur Chouilloux is here.

ROSE: Yes, sir.
(*ROSE goes out midstage left.*)

CHOUILLOUX: (*Quickly, going upstage towards FOLLAVOINE.*) Please. Don't disturb your wife.

FOLLAVOINE: It's quite all right. If I don't hurry her a little... Women are never ready.

CHOUILLOUX: I can't say the same about mine. Every morning she's the first to leave the house. The doctor's advised her to go for walks. I can't any more at my age. So her cousin goes with her.

FOLLAVOINE: (*Being polite, without thinking.*) Yes. Yes. So I've heard.

CHOUILLOUX: It suits me perfectly.

FOLLAVOINE: Yes, it... it keeps it in the family.

CHOUILLOUX: It keeps it in the family... And doesn't tire me out.
(*They laugh.*)
(*Turning round to come downstage and seeing the chamber on the desk.*) Ah! I see our agenda's on the table.

FOLLAVOINE: (*Having also come downstage.*) Ah, yes... yes.

CHOUILLOUX: (*Sure of his facts, pointing to the chamber.*) This is the chamber.

FOLLAVOINE: This is the... Yes... Yes. You recognised it?

CHOUILLOUX: (*Modestly.*) Yes. Oh... (*He is now in front of and a little to the right of the desk. He turns round and looks at the chamber.*) Well... That doesn't look at all bad... Well made...

FOLLAVOINE: Oh... Well made...

CHOUILLOUX: And unbreakable? (*He taps the chamber with a bent forefinger.*)

FOLLAVOINE: (*Going upstage of the desk.*) Unbreakable, exactly.

CHOUILLOUX: (*Contemplating it.*) Well, well... (*Suddenly, as he sits in the armchair right of the desk.*) I ask that, because it's a point that particularly attracted us... the Under Secretary of State and me.

FOLLAVOINE: Aha! Yes, yes?

CHOUILLOUX: After careful consideration we have decided we do not want ordinary china.

FOLLAVOINE: I do understand.

CHOUILLOUX: The smallest thing gets broken.

FOLLAVOINE: Immediately.

CHOUILLOUX: It would be wasting the country's money.

FOLLAVOINE: Absolutely. (*Pointing to the chamber.*) But this is reliable. It will last for ever. (*Coming downstage.*) Go on, pick it up, you're an expert.

CHOUILLOUX: Oh... not, really.

FOLLAVOINE: Yes, yes. Feel how light it is.

CHOUILLOUX: (*Taking it and feeling its weight.*) Very strange. It doesn't weigh as much as you'd think.

FOLLAVOINE: (*Taking CHOUILLOUX'S hand and shaking it to make the chamber move like a frying pan.*) And so pleasant to handle... Eh?... I mean it becomes a pleasure. (*Changing his tone.*) Of course we make them white and coloured. If you like, for example, the Army could have them striped like sentry boxes... in the national colours.

CHOUILLOUX: No, that would be pretentious.

FOLLAVOINE: I agree. And a needless increase in cost.

CHOUILLOUX: Well, well... Remarkable! Remarkable!... (*He puts it back on the desk and returns to FOLLAVOINE.*) We've also seen enamelled ones. They're not bad either.

FOLLAVOINE: No!... You can't be serious! You're not thinking of enamel!

CHOUILLOUX: Why not?

FOLLAVOINE: Because... Not because of my personal interest. I ignore that. But enamel smells from the start. And it's not clean like china. (*Pointing to the chamber.*) That's what you want.

CHOUILLOUX: Of course there are pros and cons.

FOLLAVOINE: Quite apart from the question of hygiene... You must know appendicitis is usually caused by using enamelled utensils.

CHOUILLOUX: (*Half laughing, half serious.*) Yes, but the way we're going to use them, I don't think...

FOLLAVOINE: You never know. Young men are so frivolous. They decide to christen the new article. They make an enormous punch. The heat cracks the enamel. A few pieces falls off. They're swallowed... Well, you know what happens.

CHOUILLOUX: No... No, I must say I've never happened to drink punch out of a...

FOLLAVOINE: No. But you've been a soldier.

CHOUILLOUX: Hardly. I went for my medical. They made me take all my clothes off and then said I was short-sighted. That decided my army career. I spent my whole life at the War Ministry.

FOLLAVOINE: Oh?... Well, believe me, not enamel.
Rubber, if you like. Or celluloid. But there's nothing
to compare with china. Its only defect is it fragility.
And once that's eliminated! Look, you'll see. (*Wanting
to go to the desk, but finding CHOUILLOUX in his way.*)
Excuse me.

CHOUILLOUX: (*Not understanding and moving in the same
direction.*) Excuse me.

FOLLAVOINE: (*Pointing to the chamber on the desk.*) No,
I was going to...

CHOUILLOUX: (*Drawing back to let him pass.*) Oh, excuse me.

FOLLAVOINE: (*Picking up the chamber.*) You'll see how
strong it is. (*He raises it as if to throw it, then changes his
mind.*) No, here with the carpet we'd prove nothing. But
in the hall there's a wooden floor... You'll see. (*He has
gone to the hall door and opened it. He comes down centre stage
to the footlights next to CHOUILLOUX. He then points
upstage.*) There.

(*CHOUILLOUX is about to go there.*)

(*Stopping him.*) No, stay here. Look there. (*As he is about
to throw the chamber.*) Watch carefully. (*Swinging it to get
the right momentum.*) One... two... three. (*He throws it.*)
Now... there.

(*As he says 'There', the chamber falls and shatters. They
both remain there for a moment open-mouthed with
amazement. FOLLAVOINE is still rooted to the spot, as
CHOUILLOUX makes a half circle round him to finish
facing him, slightly upstage and right, and so also facing
the audience. If the chamber fails to break, FOLLAVOINE
simply says:'You see. Unbreakable. You can throw it as many
times as you like. If you'd care to check, look. One... two...
three...' etc.*)

CHOUILLOUX: It's broken.

FOLLAVOINE: Eh?

CHOUILLOUX: It's broken.

FOLLAVOINE: Yes, it's... it's broken.

CHOUILLOUX: (*Having gone upstage to the door.*) There's
no... It's not an optical illusion?

FOLLAVOINE: (*Having gone upstage.*) No, no. It really is broken. Extraordinary. I don't understand. I swear it's never happened before.

CHOUILLOUX: (*Coming downstage.*) Perhaps there's a flaw in it.

FOLLAVOINE: (*Also coming downstage.*) Perhaps yes... Actually I'm sorry this has happened. It simply shows that... that... the exception proves the rule. Because they never never break.

CHOUILLOUX: Never?

FOLLAVOINE: Never. Or, I don't know, one in a thousand.

CHOUILLOUX: Ah! One in a thousand.

FOLLAVOINE: Yes, or... or more. I'll show you. (*Going upstage towards the bookcase.*) I've another one here. We'll throw it over and over again... (*Coming downstage with a second chamber which he has taken from the bookcase.*) Ignore that one, it was badly fired.

CHOUILLOUX: Yes, badly fired.

FOLLAVOINE: Now! (*He goes and stands centre stage at the footlights next to CHOUILLOUX, who is already there.*) Watch carefully. One... two... (*Changing his mind.*) No. You throw it. (*He gives it to him.*)

CHOUILLOUX: Me?

FOLLAVOINE: Yes. You'll get a better idea.

CHOUILLOUX: Oh?...

(*FOLLAVOINE moves away to the right. CHOUILLOUX takes his place. They remain in the same position relative to each other.*)

FOLLAVOINE: Go on.

CHOUILLOUX: Yes. (*Swinging the chamber.*) One... two... (*He stops, overcome with emotion.*)

FOLLAVOINE: Go on. Why have you stopped?

CHOUILLOUX: It's the first time I've ever played bowls with a...

FOLLAVOINE: Go on, go on. Don't be afraid. (*To calm him.*) I told you, one in a thousand.

CHOUILLOUX: One... two... and three. (*He throws it.*)

FOLLAVOINE: (*During its flight.*) Now! (*As it hits the ground.*) There!

(*The chamber breaks into pieces as before.*)
(*Same action as the last time. They both stand there as though bewitched. A pause.*)

CHOUILLOUX: (*Going upstage to inspect the damage.*) It's broken!

FOLLAVOINE: (*Having also gone upstage.*) It's broken, yes. It's broken...

CHOUILLOUX: Two in a thousand!

FOLLAVOINE: Two in a thousand, yes. Listen. I don't understand. It's something I can't explain. It must be because of the way it was thrown. I know when my foreman does it, never, absolutely never...

CHOUILLOUX: Ah! Never?

FOLLAVOINE: Never.

(*CHOUILLOUX goes and sits on the sofa, while FOLLAVOINE closes the hall door.*)

CHOUILLOUX: That's most interesting.

FOLLAVOINE: Yes... No... It's not like that... Obviously you can see the difference between breakable china and...

CHOUILLOUX: (*Finishing the sentence.*) Unbreakable china.

FOLLAVOINE: Yes... Of course these experiments aren't conclusive enough for you to reach any decision.

CHOUILLOUX: Yes, yes I quite understand... The same chamber pots as these. Except that instead of breaking, they don't break.

FOLLAVOINE: Exactly.

CHOUILLOUX: Most interesting.

(*JULIE bursts in from her room. She is dressed as before, but without her pail.*)

JULIE: Bastien! Please do come. This child's driving me mad. I can't manage it.

(*CHOUILLOUX has risen at the sound of her voice.*)

FOLLAVOINE: (*Rushing towards her and whispering quickly.*) You're out of your mind! Coming in here like this! Look at yourself! (*Pointing to CHOUILLOUX.*) Monsieur Chouilloux!

JULIE: (*Without even turning round.*) I don't give a damn for Monsieur Chouilloux.

CHOUILLOUX: Eh?

FOLLAVOINE: (*Distraught.*) No, no. Please. (*Introducing, not knowing what to do.*) Monsieur Chouilloux. My wife.

CHOUILLOUX: (*Bowing.*) How do you do.

JULIE: (*Very quickly.*) Good morning. You will forgive me appearing like this, won't you...

CHOUILLOUX: (*Very gallant.*) Please, please. It's a pleasure to see a pretty woman, whatever she's wearing.

JULIE: (*Not listening.*) Too kind. Thank you. (*To her husband.*) I can't do anything with the child. As soon as a I mention medicine...

FOLLAVOINE: Yes, that's too bad, I'm sorry. I'm busy talking to Monsieur Chouilloux. I've no time to bother about your son's medicine.

JULIE: (*Indignantly to CHOUILLOUX.*) What a father! What a father! (*She passes to the left.*)

CHOUILLOUX: (*Not knowing what to say.*) Yes... er... yes.

FOLLAVOINE: (*Commandingly.*) Please go and get dressed. I'm ashamed for you, daring to appear in this state. Have you no concern for your dignity?

JULIE: Ha! Do you think I care what I look like at a time like this!

CHOUILLOUX: (*Wanting to appear interested.*) You've a sick child?

JULIE: (*Very sadly.*) Yes, I have.

FOLLAVOINE: (*Shrugging his shoulders; to CHOUILLOUX.*) There's nothing the matter with him. Nothing.

JULIE: (*Unanswerably.*) He hasn't been this morning.

CHOUILLOUX: Oh? Oh?

FOLLAVOINE: His bowels are rather sluggish.

JULIE: He calls that nothing! He calls that nothing! Obviously he's all right.

FOLLAVOINE: The child needs a laxative, that's all.

JULIE: Yes, I know. But you give it to him if you can. That's why I'm asking you to come. But there's no risk of that! All the difficult jobs I have to do!

FOLLAVOINE: Really, anyone would think it was something serious.

CHOUILLOUX: (*Nodding his head; seriously.*) It isn't serious. All the same you mustn't trifle with this sort of thing.

JULIE: Ah! You see what he says. He knows.

FOLLAVOINE: (*Flattering him.*) Oh, really, Monsieur Chouilloux...?

CHOUILLOUX: (*As before.*) Of course... Of course... (*To JULIE.*) Is the child prone to... forgive the word... constipation?

JULIE: He has a tendency, yes.

CHOUILLOUX: Yes? Well... You must keep an eye on that. One fine day it may develop into enteritis and that's the very devil to get rid of.

JULIE: (*To her husband.*) There. You see.

CHOUILLOUX: I know what I'm talking about. I had it. For five years.

JULIE: (*Instinctively turning her head towards her room, where her child is.*) Oh! (*She turns her head back towards CHOUILLOUX.*) Poor thing!

CHOUILLOUX: (*Bowing.*) Thank you.

JULIE: What?

CHOUILLOUX: Oh! I'm sorry I thought you meant me.

JULIE: No... no.

CHOUILLOUX: Yes, five years. I caught it in the War...

JULIE: In 1870?

CHOUILLOUX: No, '98.

JULIE: (*Looking at him, dumbfounded.*) There wasn't a war in '98.

CHOUILLOUX: I was going to say 'in the War Ministry'. I'm a civil servant.

JULIE: Oh, I see.

FOLLAVOINE: Yes, because he's...

JULIE: Yes, yes I know.

CHOUILLOUX: I was always thirsty... I drank water... from anywhere... I said 'Tcha!... Microbes!... Tap water's all right for me'. And that's how I caught enteritis. I had to go to Plombières three years running.

JULIE: (*Seizing on it.*) You think Baby should go to Plombières?

CHOUILLOUX: No... no. He seems to have a constipated form of enteritis. Chatel-Guyon would suit him better. My enteritis was... Shall we sit down?
(*JULIE and CHOUILLOUX sit on the sofa.*)

FOLLAVOINE: Yes, that's very interesting. (*He goes and gets the chair next to his desk, brings it back near the sofa and sits down.*)

CHOUILLOUX: My enteritis was more, shall I say... forgive this confidence... a loose enteritis.

JULIE: Oh?... Oh?

FOLLAVOINE: (*Flattering him.*) How interesting!

CHOUILLOUX: So they prescribed Plombières. Oh! The diet!

JULIE: (*Engrossed in what interests her.*) What do they do at Chatel-Guyon?

CHOUILLOUX: (*Slightly taken aback.*) Eh?... I don't know, I've never been there. (*Returning to what interests him.*) Now at Plombières! Every morning a douche... in increasing quantities. One litre, one and a half litres...

JULIE: I don't care about that. Don't you know if Chatel-Guyon...?

CHOUILLOUX: No, I tell you, I've never been there. (*Returning to his theme.*) Once the douche was finished, I took a bath... for one hour! After that a massage...

JULIE: (*In a hurry to return to what interests her.*) Yes... Yes.

CHOUILLOUX: After that, lunch. Nothing but white food. Purées, macaroni, spaghetti, rice, semolina...

JULIE: Yes, but... at Chatel-Guyon...

FOLLAVOINE: (*Rising, annoyed.*) He keeps telling you he's never been there.

CHOUILLOUX: Yes, I'm very sorry, but...

FOLLAVOINE: He can only tell you what he did at Plombières.

JULIE: (*Very naively.*) I don't give a damn what he did at Plombières.

CHOUILLOUX: (*Taken aback.*) Oh?... I'm sorry.

JULIE: Why should I care what he did at Plombières?

Baby needs Chatel-Guyon. (*Rising.*) Monsieur
Chouilloux's an intelligent man, he understands.

CHOUILLOUX: (*As JULIE passes to the centre.*) Yes. Yes.

JULIE: He could talk about codfishing in Newfoundland.
That would be very interesting. But it has nothing to do
with Toto's health.

CHOUILLOUX: (*Conciliatory.*) Naturally. Naturally.

JULIE: I've no time to listen to stories. I've got to give
Baby his medicine.

FOLLAVOINE: (*Having had more than enough.*) All right.
Good. That's fine. Go and give it to him.

JULIE: (*Very charmingly to CHOUILLOUX.*) You will excuse
me, won't you?

CHOUILLOUX: (*Rising.*) Please. Please.

JULIE: (*Curtly to FOLLAVOINE.*) Then you won't come?
Right?

FOLLAVOINE: No. No.

JULIE: What a father! What a father!

FOLLAVOINE: Yes. That's it. Good. Do get dressed.

JULIE: Yes... What a father! (*She goes out.*)

FOLLAVOINE: (*Upstage, facing the door she has gone through.*)
Appearing like that! It's unbelievable!

CHOUILLOUX: (*Coming upstage to the centre.*) Your wife
seems very charming.

FOLLAVOINE: Eh?... Delightful, delightful. She's sometimes rather... But apart from that, delightful. You
haven't seen her properly. I'm sorry she appeared like
this, not dressed...

CHOUILLOUX: Of course I realise that with... (*He finishes
the sentence with a mime that evokes an idea of frills and
furbelows.*)

FOLLAVOINE: Yes... No... Like this with her hair down...
in curlers. Her hair is her proudest possession... Superb...
Naturally curly.

CHOUILLOUX: Oh?... Oh?

FOLLAVOINE: So when you see her like this... She's so
elegant!... But when she thinks she ought to start worrying about her son...

CHOUILLOUX: (*Coming downstage and sitting in the arm-chair in front of the desk.*) There's nothing really wrong with the child?

FOLLAVOINE: (*Coming downstage after him to the front of the desk and leaning back against it.*) Nothing... But try to tell her! You mentioned Chatel-Guyon. Now I'll hear about nothing else.

CHOUILLOUX: I'm sorry if it's my fault...

FOLLAVOINE: Not at all, not at all. But when after that you began telling her about Plombières, I nearly collapsed with laughter. (*He laughs.*)

CHOUILLOUX: (*Approvingly.*) She wasn't remotely interested.

FOLLAVOINE: (*Laughing.*) Not in the slightest.

CHOUILLOUX: Poor woman! And I was... (*He laughs.*) (*As they are both roaring with laughter the door midstage left opens suddenly and JULIE appears, dragging TOTO along with her right hand. She has a wine glass in her left hand and is clasping a bottle of Hunyadi-Janos to her chest.*)

JULIE: Just you come along and see your father. (*She releases TOTO to close the door, then immediately seizes his hand again and drags him towards his father, still talking.*) Daddy's furious with you. (*Having reached FOLLAVOINE.*) Will you tell your son... (*She sees he is still laughing with CHOUILLOUX and kicks him in the shin. She pushes TOTO away and whispers so he won't hear.*) Stop it.

FOLLAVOINE: (*Jumping in agony.*) For God's sake!

JULIE: I told Toto you were furious with him. If he sees you roaring with laughter...

FOLLAVOINE: What's the matter now?

JULIE: (*Giving him TOTO.*) The matter is making your son do what he's told. So will *you* give him his medicine! (*She reaches the left.*)

FOLLAVOINE: Me?

JULIE: Yes, you. (*Putting the bottle and then the glass on the small table near the sofa.*) Here's the bottle. Here's the glass. I'll have nothing more to do with it.

FOLLAVOINE: It's not my job. What's it got to do with me?

JULIE: You're his father, It's up to you to use your authority.

FOLLAVOINE: (*Raising his eyes to heaven, then to CHOUILLOUX with a sigh of resignation.*) Do forgive me..

CHOUILLOUX: Please, please.

FOLLAVOINE: (*Severely to TOTO.*) What's this sir? I'm very annoyed.

TOTO: (*Stamping his foot and passing between his father and CHOUILLOUX.*) I don't care. I won't drink it.

FOLLAVOINE: What?

JULIE: (*On edge.*) There! I've heard nothing else for the last half hour.

CHOUILLOUX: (*Putting his hand on TOTO'S shoulder in a friendly way.*) What's this!... A big boy like you! (*TOTO angrily shakes him off.*)

FOLLAVOINE: What did I see?... To start with, say how do you do.

TOTO: (*Stubbornly stamping his foot.*) I don't care. I won't drink it.

FOLLAVOINE: (*Shaking him.*) Won't drink it! You horrid little child...

JULIE: (*Jumping at FOLLAVOINE and pulling him sharply away.*) What do you think you're up to?

FOLLAVOINE: Oh hell! (*He angrily goes upstage, then comes down again to his desk but does not sit down.*)

JULIE: (*To CHOUILLOUX.*) We can't not give him his medicine. His tongue's all white. (*To TOTO.*) Show the gentleman your tongue.

CHOUILLOUX: (*Obligingly.*) Just a moment. (*He puts one knee on the ground to be the same height as TOTO and takes a pair of pince nez from his waistcoat pocket. He then puts them on his nose above his spectacles. To TOTO.*) Can I see?

JULIE: Let him see your tongue. (*TOTO puts out his tongue which is black with ink.*)

CHOUILLOUX: Good heavens! It seems to be... black.

JULIE: (*With a certain pride.*) That's because he's been doing his homework... (*Changing her tone.*) But you can easily tell his breath's bad.(*To TOTO, pushing his head into CHOUILLOUX'S face.*) Blow in the gentleman's face.

CHOUILLOUX: (*Instinctively protecting himself with his hand.*). No, thank you, no.

JULIE: You don't mind the breath of a child?

CHOUILLOUX: Not at all. Not at all. But...

JULIE: Well then? (*To TOTO, once again pushing his head into CHOUILLOUX'S face.*) Go on, blow in the gentleman's face.

CHOUILLOUX: No, no. I assure you it's quite unnecessary. I can tell... (*To TOTO, sitting down.*) What's the matter then? Do you call this being sensible?... What's your name?

(*Sulky gesture from TOTO, who doesn't answer.*)

FOLLAVOINE: (*Leaning across the desk.*) Go on, tell him. What's your name?

TOTO: (*Obstinately.*) I won't drink it.

FOLLAVOINE: (*Champing at the bit.*) Ohhh! (*Amicably to CHOUILLOUX.*) His name's Toto.

CHOUILLOUX: Ah?

FOLLAVOINE: Short for Hervé.

CHOUILLOUX: Really?... How strange!... How old are you? Six?

JULIE: (*Importantly.*) Seven.

CHOUILLOUX: Is that so! Seven! And your name's Toto! Well when we're seven and our name's Toto, we don't make a fuss about a little medicine, do we?

TOTO: I don't care. I won't drink it.

CHOUILLOUX: That's very bad. What will you say when you're older and you have to go to war?

JULIE: (*Quickly pulling TOTO to her, as if to protect him and superstitiously tapping three times with her left hand on the wood of the desk.*) Sh!

TOTO: (*In his mother's skirts.*) I don't care. I won't go to war.

CHOUILLOUX: Won't go! Won't go! If there is a war, you'll have to...

TOTO: I don't care. I'll go to Belgium.

CHOUILLOUX: Eh?

JULIE: (*Covering him with kisses.*) My darling!... Isn't he clever!

CHOUILLOUX: (*To FOLLAVOINE.*) Congratulations! Did *you* bring him up with these ideas?

FOLLAVOINE: (*Quickly.*) No, no. (*To TOTO.*) It's very naughty saying things like that... Do you hear?... Hervé?

JULIE: (*Taking TOTO towards the sofa.*) Leave the poor child alone. Don't upset him with grown-up things. (*Sitting on the sofa with TOTO between her knees.*) He's a clever, sensible boy and he's going to please his mummy by taking his medicine. (*As she was talking, she filled the glass and on the word 'medicine' offers it to TOTO.*)

TOTO: (*Breaking away from her.*) I won't drink it.

JULIE: But we tell you you must.

FOLLAVOINE: (*Coming to the chair next to the sofa and sitting.*) Look, Toto. If you'd obeyed right away, it would all be over now.

TOTO: I don't care. I won't.

FOLLAVOINE: Will you be sensible!

TOTO: (*Breaking away and going to the right.*) No, I won't.

CHOUILLOUX: (*Having risen, intervening.*) My dear boy, when I was your age... and my parents told me to do something, then...

TOTO: (*Into his face.*) Silly old fool!

FOLLAVOINE and JULIE: Oh!

CHOUILLOUX: (*Taken aback.*) What?

FOLLAVOINE: (*Jumping at TOTO and pushing him behind him.*) Nothing, nothing.

CHOUILLOUX: (*Accepting the position.*) Oh! I'm sorry. (*He goes and sits in the armchair at the right of the desk.*)

FOLLAVOINE: (*Furiously shaking TOTO.*) Will you do what you're told! You horrid little...

JULIE: (*Intervening and snatching the child away.*) You must be mad! You're not going to hit the child?

FOLLAVOINE: Didn't you hear? He said 'Silly old fool'!

JULIE: Yes, he said 'Silly old fool'. He's right, isn't he?

FOLLAVOINE: (*Indignant.*) Oh!

JULIE: (*To TOTO, embracing him.*) My poor darling! (*She takes him to the sofa and sits.*)

FOLLAVOINE: (*Going upstage to his desk.*) Damn, damn, damn! (*He sits down angrily.*)

JULIE: (*To TOTO clutching him in her right arm and caressing his cheek with hers.*) Your father's a wicked man. But never mind, mummy's here.

FOLLAVOINE: (*Furious.*) There you go! Putting ideas into his head!

JULIE: (*Taking the full glass from the small table in her right hand and passing it into her left.*) I'm right... Ill-treating this poor sick child!

FOLLAVOINE: (*Turning his chair round so that his back is almost to the desk, as if trying to remain aloof.*) From now on I'll have nothing more to do with it.

JULIE: (*Rudely.*) Good. (*To TOTO, immediately becoming very charming as she puts the glass to his lips.*) Take your medicine, darling. Like a man!

TOTO: (*With set lips, turning his head away.*) No, I won't.

JULIE: (*Her nostrils dilated, her lips set, looking furiously at her husband, then controlling herself and turning back towards TOTO; pleading.*) Yes... To please me.

TOTO: (*Obstinate.*) No, I won't.

JULIE: (*As before, looking at her husband, then turning back to TOTO.*) Please, darling, take your medicine.

TOTO: No!

JULIE: (*Clenching her teeth.*) Ohhh! (*Casting a look of hatred at FOLLAVOINE.*) When you start interfering...!

FOLLAVOINE: (*Dumbfounded.*) Me!

JULIE: Of course, you. (*To TOTO.*) Listen, Toto. If you take your medicine, Mummy will give you a sweet.

TOTO: No, I want the sweet first.

JULIE: No, afterwards.

TOTO: No, first.

JULIE: Oh!... All right. I'll give you the sweet first. But afterwards you will take your medicine?

TOTO: Yes.

JULIE: You promise?

TOTO: Yes.

JULIE: You give me your word of honour?

TOTO: (*A long drawn-out yes.*) Yes.

JULIE: Very well, I trust you. (*To FOLLAVOINE, who is sitting at his desk, his back almost turned, his eyes on the ceiling, in a resigned attitude.*) Daddy! (*Seeing he is not paying attention and does not answer; curtly.*) Bastien!

CHOUILLOUX: (*Automatically.*) Bastien!

FOLLAVOINE: (*As if coming out of a dream.*) Eh?

JULIE: (*Curtly.*) The sweets!

CHOUILLOUX: (*Passing on the request.*) The sweets!

FOLLAVOINE: (*The victim; sighing.*) Here they are. (*He has opened the drawer in his desk and taken out a box of sweets. He rises and, as he is about to take it to JULIE, says to CHOUILLOUX.*) I'm so sorry you've had to witness this little family scene.

CHOUILLOUX: Not at all. It's very interesting... for a man with no children.

FOLLAVOINE: (*Handing the open box of sweets to JULIE.*) Here are the sweets.

JULIE: (*Taking one.*) Thank you. (*To TOTO.*) Open your mouth, darling. (*Putting a sweet in his mouth.*) There!

FOLLAVOINE: (*Putting the box back in the drawer; to CHOUILLOUX.*) I didn't ask you to lunch for this.

CHOUILLOUX: (*Unconcerned.*) Oh...

JULIE: (*To TOTO.*) Was it nice?

TOTO: Yes.

JULIE: (*Holding out the glass.*) Good. Now, darling, drink it up. Take your medicine.

TOTO: (*Escaping.*) No, I won't.

JULIE: (*Dumbfounded.*) What?

FOLLAVOINE: (*His nerves on edge.*) You see, dammit! You see!

JULIE: Now, Toto, you're not being sensible. I gave you a sweet.

TOTO: (*Going upstage.*) I don't care, I won't drink it.

FOLLAVOINE: (*Controlling himself with difficulty.*) That child! That child!

JULIE: (*Furiously to FOLLAVOINE, as she goes to TOTO.*) What do you mean; 'That child!'? Going on saying 'That child! That child!', instead of helping! You can see it's got beyond me. (*She picks up TOTO under the armpits, takes him over to the sofa and sits down.*)

FOLLAVOINE: (*Losing his temper.*) What do you expect me to do?

JULIE: (*Going upstage centre.*) Nothing, nothing. Naturally. (*Bitterly.*) Ohhh! (*She goes towards the door of her room.*)

FOLLAVOINE: Well, what then? What? Where are you going?

JULIE: Where do you think? I'm going to try something else. (*Having reached the door, she turns round and points to CHOUILLOUX.*) And today of all days he asks people to lunch!

(*JULIE goes out, slamming the door.*)

FOLLAVOINE: (*Leaping in the air; under his breath.*) Ohhh!

CHOUILLOUX: (*Having also risen.*) What?

FOLLAVOINE: (*Innocently.*) Eh?

CHOUILLOUX: What did your wife say?

FOLLAVOINE: Nothing, nothing... She said: 'I really don't know when we'll have lunch'.

CHOUILLOUX: (*Unconcerned, sitting down again.*) Oh?... Never mind...

FOLLAVOINE: (*Going to TOTO and taking his hand to make him get up.*) It's naughty, Toto, breaking your word like that... Isn't it, Monsieur Chouilloux?

CHOUILLOUX: (*Prudent.*) I'm not saying another word. Not another word.

FOLLAVOINE: (*Squatting down in front of TOTO, to be the same height.*) Look, Toto. You're seven. You're a young man. You can't behave like a child now... If you're good and take your medicine, I'll give you a surprise. (*He stands up.*)

TOTO: (*Curious.*) What?

FOLLAVOINE: I'll tell you where the Urals are.

TOTO: I don't care, I don't want to know.

FOLLAVOINE: That's naughty. (*Under his breath.*) Especially after the trouble we've had finding them. (*To TOTO.*). They're between Europe and Asia.

TOTO: (*Not caring.*) Oh?

(*FOLLAVOINE releases him and turning on his heels, reaches the right.*)

(*TOTO catches him by the tail of his coat.*)
And Lake Michigan?

FOLLAVOINE: (*Frowning.*) What?

TOTO: Where's Lake Michigan?

FOLLAVOINE: (*Repeating automatically.*) Where's Lake
Michigan?

TOTO: Yes.

FOLLAVOINE: I heard... (*Aside.*) He's infuriating with
these damned questions. (*To CHOUILLOUX.*) Tell me...
I was wondering... Lake Michigan... Do you by any
chance recall where it is?

CHOUILLOUX: Lake Michigan?

FOLLAVOINE: Yes.

CHOUILLOUX: It's in America... The United States.

FOLLAVOINE: How stupid of me! Of course.

CHOUILLOUX: In the State of Michigan.

FOLLAVOINE: Of Michigan! That's it! I couldn't remember
the name of the State.

CHOUILLOUX: Lake Michigan. In '77 I swam in it.

FOLLAVOINE: You did?... (*Leaning towards TOTO and
pointing to CHOUILLOUX.*) You see, Toto. You were
looking for Lake Michigan and this gentleman... who
looks perfectly ordinary... swam in it! (*Straight on.*) After
that I hope you'll be sensible and take your medicine.

TOTO: (*Escaping and climbing onto the sofa.*) No, I won't.

FOLLAVOINE: (*Raising his eyes to heaven.*) Ohhh!

CHOUILLOUX: He's a determined child.

FOLLAVOINE: (*With feeling.*) Yes, he is.

(*JULIE enters, carrying a second glass, similar to the first,
and comes downstage extreme left to the small table.*)

JULIE: I've brought another glass... (*Filling it with the
medicine.*) And so that Baby will be a good boy and
drink his medicine... (*Putting the bottle down and collecting
TOTO, going with him to FOLLAVOINE, right.*) Daddy will
drink a big glass with him.

FOLLAVOINE: (*With a start.*) What?

JULIE: (*To FOLLAVOINE, thrusting the glass into his face.*)
Won't you?

FOLLAVOINE: (*Taking refuge behind his desk.*) I certainly won't. Thank you very much.

JULIE: (*Curtly, half whisper.*) For my sake. You won't say no?

FOLLAVOINE: Oh yes, I will. I don't need it. Drink it yourself, if you're so keen.

JULIE: You won't even do this for your son?

FOLLAVOINE: (*Pushing away the glass which JULIE is stubbornly putting to his lips.*) My son! My son! He's yours too.

JULIE: Is that so? What about all the work then? (*Putting the glass down on the corner of the desk.*) Yes, work. Do you think I haven't done enough for him since he was born?... And before that... Do you think it's not enough to have carried him for nine months...? (*She passes in front of TOTO and comes downstage left a little.*)

FOLLAVOINE: (*Annoyed.*) Carried him! What are you getting at? (*He sits at his desk.*)

TOTO: Mummy?

JULIE: What?

TOTO: Why did you carry me? Why not Daddy?

JULIE: (*Picking him up, going to the sofa, putting him on it and sitting down next to him.*) Why?... Because your father... If you had to rely on him!... But he knew I had to, so... that was that.

FOLLAVOINE: (*To CHOUILLOUX.*) I ask you! Is this the sort of thing to tell a child!

TOTO: You should have taken another man.

FOLLAVOINE: (*Furious.*) You should have taken another man! Charming!

JULIE: Well... they're all alike...

TOTO: I won't be like that.

JULIE: (*Embracing him.*) Darling! You love me anyway.

FOLLAVOINE: (*To CHOUILLOUX.*) She's mad. Mad!

CHOUILLOUX: No, it's charming. (*Rising and considering TOTO from afar.*) The things children think of!

JULIE: (*To TOTO.*) You see the difference between a father and a mother! Your father won't even take a little medicine for you!

TOTO: I don't care. I don't want him to.

FOLLAVOINE: (*Coming downstage to the sofa.*) Well, well!...
Do you hear? He's more sensible than you are.

CHOUILLOUX: (*Also coming downstage towards TOTO.*)
well, well!... He doesn't want his Daddy to drink it!

TOTO: (*Pointing to CHOUILLOUX.*) I want this gentleman
to.

FOLLAVOINE: Eh?

CHOUILLOUX: (*Recoiling instinctively.*) What?

JULIE: (*Happy to seize this opportunity of pleasing her son.*) You
want this gentleman to? Then this gentleman will. (*She
takes the full glass from the small table and, with TOTO
clinging to her, goes towards CHOUILLOUX.*)

FOLLAVOINE: (*Intervening.*) You can't do that!

JULIE: (*Pushing him aside and passing across with TOTO.*)
Leave me alone.

CHOUILLOUX: (*Centre stage at the footlights, grumbling
under his breath.*) What an ill-mannered little brat! Oh!

JULIE: (*Holding the glass.*) Here you are, dear Monsieur
Chouilloux.
(*She puts the glass to his lips as he says '...little brat! Oh!', so
that in taking a breath on the 'Oh', he accidentally swallows
a mouthful.*)

CHOUILLOUX: Oh! Pah!

JULIE: (*Accompanied by TOTO, advancing on CHOUILLOUX,
the glass in her outstretched hand.*) Be nice. Drink a little to
please Toto. (*Once again she puts the glass to his lips.*)

CHOUILLOUX: (*Spitting.*) Oh! (*Drawing back towards the right
as JULIE advances on him.*) No, really. No, thank you.

FOLLAVOINE: You're out of your mind!

JULIE: (*To CHOUILLOUX.*) It's such a tiny little thing. Half
a glass will be enough.
(*Same play with the glass. CHOUILLOUX struggles to
defend himself.*)

CHOUILLOUX: No, no, please!... I'm terribly sorry...

FOLLAVOINE: You must be mad! He hasn't come here
for a laxative!

JULIE: A little medicine's nothing to make a fuss about.

CHOUILLOUX: (*Driven back against the armchair right.*)
That may be, but...

JULIE: I can understand with a child, but a grown up!...
(*Winningly.*) Monsieur Chouilloux... (*She puts the glass
under his nose.*)

FOLLAVOINE: Julie, please.

CHOUILLOUX: No, no. I'm very sorry, but a laxative!
I told you about my bowels.

FOLLAVOINE: Of course.

JULIE: I know, but half a glass isn't going to harm them.

FOLLAVOINE: Julie! Julie!

JULIE: And really between Toto's health and your bowels,
I think...

FOLLAVOINE: Julie! For heaven's sake!

CHOUILLOUX: Anyway... I don't know how much your
son needs a laxative...

JULIE: (*Quickly making TOTO move to the centre; under her breath.*)
No, please!... If you're going to start saying things like that
in front of the child! That's the last straw!

FOLLAVOINE: (*Making TOTO move to the left.*) Julie! Julie!

CHOUILLOUX: I'm sorry, I only said...

JULIE: (*Into CHOUILLOUX's face.*) You've seen all the
trouble I've had with Baby. All the tact I've had to use...

FOLLAVOINE: Julie! Julie!

JULIE: (*Relentlessly.*) And now you tell him he doesn't have
to take it.

CHOUILLOX: No. No. I merely thought...

JULIE: (*Almost biting his nose off.*) Ha! You thought! You
thought!

FOLLAVOINE: Julie! Julie!

JULIE: What do you know about it? Where did you learn?
Plombières? That's the opposite.

CHOUILLOUX: All right. I'll keep out of this.

FOLLAVOINE: Listen, Julie, that's enough.

JULIE: (*Reaching the extreme left.*) So he should! I don't
interfere when his wife and her cousin Truchet make
him a cuckold. (*She puts the glass down on the small table.*)

CHOUILLOUX: (*Leaping in the air.*) Cuckold!

FOLLAVOINE: (*Under his breath.*) Oh, my God!

Not worrying anymore about CHOUILLOUX, JULIE has picked up TOTO and sat him down on the sofa, centre. She then sits next to him, left.

CHOUILLOUX: What did you say?... A cuckold!... My wife... and Truchet!

FOLLAVOINE: It's not true... It's not true.

CHOUILLOUX: (*Pushing him away.*) Leave me alone. Leave me alone. Oh!... I'm choking. (*He sees the glass which JULIE originally put on the desk, pounces on it and greedily swallows all the contents.*)

FOLLAVOINE: Oh!

TOTO: (*Delighted, pointing to CHOUILLOUX.*) Mummy! Mummy! (*He skips upstage above the desk and climbs up to kneel on his father's chair.*)

JULIE: (*Not moving, to CHOUILLOUX as he swallows the medicine.*) Well!... Couldn't you have done that right away?... Instead of making all this fuss!

FOLLAVOINE: (*Distraught.*) Monsieur Chouilloux, please. (*CHOUILLOUX's face suddenly contracts and his eyes look wild. He is feeling sick. He looks distractedly to right and left, then suddenly remembering where FOLLAVOINE kept the chambers, he rushes madly towards the bookcase upstage right.*)
(*Reading his thoughts and running after him.*) No, not in there! There aren't any more. There aren't any more. (*Pushing him towards the door downstage left.*) Through there. Look. Through there.
(*CHOUILLOUX rushes out downstage right.*)
(*Closing the door and turning round towards his wife.*) Congratulations! Look what you've done.

JULIE: (*Rising and reaching the right.*) He shouldn't interfere in other people's business.

FOLLAVOINE: (*Reaching midstage.*) Telling the poor man he's a cuckold! (*He goes upstage.*)

JULIE: (*Sitting in the armchair, right of the desk.*) You mean he isn't?

FOLLAVOINE: (*Turning round and coming back downstage.*) There's no need to tell him! (*He goes upstage left.*)

TOTO: Mummy!

JULIE: Yes, darling. You want your medicine?

TOTO: No... What's a cuckold?

JULIE: (*With a sarcastic smile.*) Oh... (*Pointing to the door downstage left.*) That gentleman is. The one who's just gone out.

FOLLAVOINE: (*Not having stopped walking up and down, turning round sharply.*) No, no, no!... What a thing to say to a child!

JULIE: He should have drunk it up right away, as I asked him to.

FOLLAVOINE: You are marvellous! A laxative! (*He goes upstage.*)

JULIE: Well...when you're a guest, you drink what you're given. He's no manners, your Chouilloux. He comes here for the first time and starts talking about his bowels... Where was he brought up?

FOLLAVOINE: (*Coming back downstage centre.*) You asked him to clear his bowels out!

JULIE: (*Rising and going towards him.*) I asked him to clear his bowels out? I don't give a damn about his bowels. I only asked him to drink a glass of medicine. (*She moves across upstage of the desk, collecting TOTO as she goes, and comes downstage with him on the extreme right.*)

FOLLAVOINE: But that will clear his bowels out.

JULIE: (*Sitting in the armchair right of the desk, with TOTO between her knees.*) That's his concern. Anyway, what does it matter? He drank it in the end. So why make such a fuss?

(*The bell rings off.*)

FOLLAVOINE: Think what it will do to me... and the Army contract.

JULIE: That's all you think about.

FOLLAVOINE: (*Upstage of the sofa.*) How am I going to calm him down?

(*ROSE enters.*)

ROSE: (*Announcing.*) Madame Chouilloux! Monsieur Truchet!

FOLLAVOINE: No, no, no! You receive them. I couldn't bear the sight of them now. (*He goes towards the door downstage left.*)

JULIE: (*Rising.*) No! No! Bastien!... I don't know them.

FOLLAVOINE: I don't care. Sort it out yourself.

(*FOLLAVOINE goes out. MADAME CHOUILLOUX sweeps in, followed by TRUCHET.*)

MADAME CHOUILLOUX: Madame Follavoine, I presume?

JULIE: (*Against the left corner of the desk; taken aback.*) Eh?... No... Yes.

(*TOTO hides behind JULIE, holding a piece of her dressing gown in front of him.*)

MADAME CHOUILLOUX: Ah! Delighted to meet you. (*Alluding to JULIE's dress.*) I was afraid we were going to be late. I see we're not.

JULIE: (*Embarrassed.*) No... No... Forgive me, I... I haven't had time to get dressed...

MADAME CHOUILLOUX: Please! There's no need to be formal... (*Introducing.*) Monsieur Truchet, my cousin, you very kindly asked him.

TRUCHET: I'm embarrassed to arrive like this... the first time I've had the honour...

JULIE: Please...

MADAME CHOUILLOUX: (*Seeing TOTO's head peeping out behind the dressing gown.*) And this is yours... this sweet little girl?

JULIE: (*Releasing TOTO.*) Yes... yes. But it's a boy.

MADAME CHOUILLOUX: (*Taken aback.*) Oh? (*As an excuse.*) At this age, don't you agree... there's no way of telling?

JULIE: That's right, yes... yes.

TRUCHET: Your husband's not here?

JULIE: (*Pointing to the door downstage left.*) Yes. Yes, there... in there.

TOTO: (*Artlessly putting his foot in it.*) With the cuckold.

JULIE: (*Quickly pushing TOTO behind her.*) Oh!

MADAME CHOUILLOUX: (*Wondering if she's heard correctly.*) What?

JULIE: (*Quickly.*) Nothing. nothing. It's... It's one of my husband's clerks.

MADAME CHOUILLOUX: Poor man! (*Going straight on.*) That reminds me, is my husband here?

JULIE: Yes... Yes, of course. In there.

MADAME CHOUILLOUX: Oh?... With them.

JULIE: Them?

TRUCHET: Your husband and the cuckold.

JULIE: Oh!... Yes... Yes, yes... Do sit down, please. Do
sit down.

> (*MADAME CHOUILLOUX goes and sits on the sofa, left,
> while TRUCHET goes upstage to get the upright chair. At
> this moment the door downstage left opens and
> CHOUILLOUX bursts in, followed by FOLLAVOINE. They
> are both talking at once.*)

FOLLAVOINE: I promise you...

CHOUILLOUX: Leave me alone. Leave me alone.

MADAME CHOUILLOUX: (*Advancing towards him.*) Ah!
Antoine!

CHOUILLOUX: How dare you!

TRUCHET and MADAME CHOUILLOUX: (*Dumbfounded.*) What?

FOLLAVOINE: (*Above the sofa.*) Ohhh!

CHOUILLOUX: (*Pointing to his wife.*) Look at her. My
adulterous wife!

MADAME CHOUILLOUX: Me?

CHOUILLOUX: (*Going to TRUCHET and pointing at him.*)
And look at him. My treacherous friend!

TRUCHET: My dear fellow!

CHOUILLOUX: (*Having reached centre stage, taking off his
morning coat and sticking his chest out.*) And look at me.
The cuckold!

FOLLAVOINE: (*From behind them, joining CHOUILLOUX
centre stage.*) Ohhh!

MADAME CHOUILLOUX: You're mad, my dear, mad.

TRUCHET: Whoever told you... ?

CHOUILLOUX: Who told me? (*Pointing to FOLLAVOINE
on his right.*) Ask him. (*Pointing to JULIE on his left.*) Ask her.

FOLLAVOINE: It's not true. It's not true.

MADAME CHOUILLOUX: (*Going to towards her husband.*)
My dear...

CHOUILLOUX: (*Thrusting her away.*) Leave me alone. I never want to see you again. (*To TRUCHET.*) As for you, sir, my seconds will call on you. (*He goes upstage and takes his hat.*)

MADAME CHOUILLOUX: (*Rushing after him.*) My dear, please listen...

TRUCHET: (*Also going upstage.*) My dear fellow...

CHOUILLOUX: No!

(*CHOUILLOUX goes out, followed by his wife.*)

TRUCHET: (*Coming downstage and going straight to FOLLAVOINE.*) You said that?

FOLLAVOINE: No there's a misunderstanding.

TRUCHET: Very well. You'll give me satisfaction. (*He slaps his face.*)

FOLLAVOINE: (*Seeing stars.*) Oh, my God!...

TRUCHET: I expect to hear from your seconds. (*TRUCHET goes out, furious.*)

FOLLAVOINE: (*Dabbing at his cheek.*) Ohhh!

JULIE: (*After a pause, looking at him scornfully with her hands on her hips.*) Well? Are you satisfied? See what you've got us into?

FOLLAVOINE: (*Dumbfounded.*) Me!... Me!... You dare to say I did!

JULIE: (*Shrugging her shoulders.*) Of course you did. You asked them to lunch.

FOLLAVOINE: It's all my fault?

JULIE: Oh, leave me in peace. You'll never do it again. (*JULIE goes out furiously midstage left.*)

FOLLAVOINE: It's all my fault! My fault! I've a duel because of her and it's my fault! (*Collapsing on the sofa.*) That woman will drive me out of my mind! (*Choking with indignation, he sees the other glass of medicine on the small table next to him. He pounces on it and swallows it all in a single draught.*)

TOTO: (*Watching him; aside, delighted.*) Ohhh!

FOLLAVOINE: Ohhh! Pah!

(*FOLLAVOINE rushes out like a madman, downstage left.*)

TOTO: (*Happily snapping his fingers.*) Lovely! Lovely! (*He goes to the small table, picks up the glass, turns it upside down, then shakes it like a bell, to make sure it is really empty. Then he snaps his fingers again.*) Lovely! Lovely! (*Holding the empty glass, he runs to the door midstage left and opens it half way.*) Mummy!... Mummy!

JULIE: (*Off.*) Yes. What is it?

TOTO: Mummy! Come here. (*He comes downstage centre.*) (*JULIE enters and goes to him.*)

JULIE: What do you want darling?

TOTO: (*With disconcerting impudence.*) Look... I've drunk it. (*He holds out the glass.*)

JULIE: What?

TOTO: (*Turning the glass upside down to show that it's empty.*) The medicine!

JULIE: (*Kneeling down next to him.*) You've drunk it! Darling, you are a good boy! You see. It wasn't so terrible.

TOTO: (*With a malicious smile.*) Oh, no. (*FOLLAVOINE bursts in, wearing his hat and overcoat.*)

FOLLAVOINE: I can't stand any more. I'd rather leave the house for good. (*He goes to his desk, picks up some papers and angrily puts them in a file.*)

JULIE: (*Not noticing the state he's in.*) Bastien! Baby's drunk his medicine.

FOLLAVOINNE: I don't give a damn. (*FOLLAVOINE goes out, furious.*)

JULIE: (*Indignant.*) He doesn't give a damn!... He doesn't give a damn! (*To TOTO.*) There's your father for you! He doesn't give a damn! Ah! Luckily you've got a mother! Lover her all you can, darling. Love her all you can. (*She smothers him with kisses.*)

Curtain

DON'T WALK ABOUT
WITH NOTHING ON

Mais n'te promène donc pas toute nue

Characters

VENTROUX, a deputy

CLARISSE, his wife

VICTOR, their manservant

AUGUSTE, (who is not seen) their son

PHARTILLON, the mayor of Moussagnac

DE JAIVAL, a journalist from *Le Figaro*

*T*he VENTROUX's *drawing room in Paris. About 1910.
Upstage centre, a double door, opening inwards, the right hand
leaf with a bolt on the outside. This door opens into the hall, on the
other side of which, immediately opposite, is the front door of the
flat, which itself opens onto the landing. On the right of the door
into the hall, a single door opens into the passage leading to
CLARISSE's room. Downstage left, a wall supporting a piece of
furniture. Midstage, a wall at an angle with a panelled double
door, leading to VENTROUX's study. Downstage right, the fireplace
with ornaments on the mantelpiece and mirror above. Midstage, a
big window, with a fanlight. Between the curtains and window, a
big lace curtain on a rail, manipulated by a cord on the left.*

*Facing the audience, a big sofa with a high back, the right arm
almost touching the far side of the mantelpiece. In front of the sofa,
right, a small table, with coffee pot, cup and sugar bowl on a tray.
Downstage, near the fireplace, a small armchair with a low back,
facing upstage. On the left of the stage, at right angles to the audience,
is a large table with a chair on each side of it. A chair right and left
of the hall door. A bell push next to the mantelpiece, upstage. A
memo pad on the table. Chandelier, fire screen, firedogs. Other
furniture as desired.*

*When the curtain rises, VICTOR is on a pair of steps, attending
to the curtain cord. The left side of the door into the hall is open.
Offstage in CLARISSE's room can be heard snatches of conversation; the voices of VENTROUX and his son are in the foreground,
with CLARISSE's voice fainter as though coming from another room.
After a moment we can make out the following.*

VENTROUX: (*Off.*) What? What did you say, Clarisse?
  (*CLARISSE's voice can be heard, too far away for the words
  to be distinguishable.*)
VENTROUX: (*Off.*) I don't know. As soon as Parliament
  rises, we'll go to Deauville.
TOTO: (*Off.*) Yes, father, yes! Deauville!
VENTROUX: (*Off.*) All right. Just wait for the session to end.
CLARISSE: (*Off, at the same level as the others.*) One moment
  darlings, while I get my nightdress.
VENTROUX: (*Off.*) Clarisse! Clarisse! You're out of your
  mind!

CLARISSE: (*Off.*) Why?

VENTROUX: (*Off.*) Look at yourself. Your son's here.

CLARISSE: (*Off.*) Yes, I know. Just let me get my night-dress.

VENTROUX: (*Off.*) No, no, no! For heaven's sake! You must be mad! We can see you. Go away.

CLARISSE: (*Off.*) Don't be so boring. If you must make a scene...

VENTROUX: (*Off.*) No! *I'll* go. Rather than see you... Auguste! Why do you have to stay in your mother's room?

(*VICTOR has stopped work to listen.*)

VICTOR: (*Shaking his head.*) They're fighting again.

VENTROUX: (*Off.*) Get the hell out of here.

HIS SON: (*Off.*) Yes, father.

(*VENTROUX enters, slamming the door behind him.*)

VENTROUX: She has no idea of decency... (*To VICTOR.*) What are you doing here?

VICTOR: (*Still on the steps.*) I'm mending the curtain cord.

VENTROUX: Can't you go away, when you hear me... hear me talking to my wife?

VICTOR: I wanted to finish it, sir.

VENTROUX: Yes. So you could listen at the door?

VICTOR: Door!... I'm at the window.

VENTROUX: All right, go away.

VICTOR: (*Abandoning the curtain, leaving it drawn back, and coming down from the steps.*) Yes, sir. (*He rotates the lower part of the steps so that he can fold them up.*)

VENTROUX: And take your steps with you.

VICTOR: Yes sir.

(*VICTOR goes out with the steps.*)

VENTROUX: (*Angrily closing the door after him.*) He always has to be where he's not wanted. (*He comes downstage and sulkily sits at the right of the table.*)

(*CLARISSE bursts in from her room. She is in a nightdress, but still wearing her hat and boots.*)

CLARISSE: (*Coming downstage towards her husband.*) Will you please tell me what's got into you! Who's upset you now?

VENTROUX: (*His right elbow on the table, his chin in the palm of his hand; without turning round.*) Obviously the person who's asking. (*Turning round towards her and seeing what she is wearing.*) No, no, no! On top of everything else you're not going to walk round the flat in your night-dress... with your hat on!

CLARISSE: Yes, well... First of all give me an explanation. I'll take my hat off later.

VENTROUX: Hat! I don't give a damn about your hat. That's not what's wrong.

CLARISSE: What have I done?

VENTROUX: Nothing. Nothing. You never do anything.

CLARISSE: (*Going upstage towards the sofa.*) I don't see...

VENTROUX: (*Rising.*) That's worse. It's much more serious, if you've no idea what you've done.

CLARISSE: (*Sitting on the sofa.*) When you condescend to tell me...

VENTROUX: (*He spells it out.*) You really thing it's proper for a mother to put on her nightdress in front of her son?

CLARISSE: That's the reason for this outburst?

VENTROUX: Of course it is.

CLARISSE: Really! I thought I'd committed a crime.

VENTROUX: Well you think you're behaving correctly?

CLARISSE: (*Unconcerned.*) What does it matter? Auguste's a child. He doesn't look. With your mother it doesn't count.

VENTROUX: That's not the point. It isn't done. (*He goes upstage above the sofa.*)

CLARISSE: A child of twelve!

VENTROUX: (*Behind her.*) I'm sorry, thirteen.

CLARISSE: No, twelve.

VENTROUX: Thirteen, I tell you. Three days ago.

CLARISSE: All right, three days ago. That doesn't count.

VENTROUX: (*Coming downstage centre.*) Nothing counts with you.

CLARISSE: He doesn't even know what a woman is.

VENTROUX: It's not for you to teach him. Why do you always walk about with nothing on?

CLARISSE: Nothing on? I'd my underclothes.

VENTROUX: That's even more indecent. You can be seen through them like tracing paper.

CLARISSE: (*Rising and going towards him.*) So that's it. Go on, say it. That's what you mean. You want me to wear calico.

VENTROUX: (*Dumbfounded.*) Calico? Who ever mentioned calico?

CLARISSE: I'm extremely sorry, but all women in my position have lace underwear. I don't see why mine should be red flannel. (*As she speaks, she moves to the left.*)

VENTROUX: (*Coming downstage right.*) Splendid! It's red flannel now!

CLARISSE: What would people say?

VENTROUX: (*Turning round.*) People! What people? Are you going to start displaying your underwear?

CLARISSE: (*Turning round sharply and marching on him.*) Displaying my underwear! You accuse me of displaying my underwear! That's what you descend to!

VENTROUX: (*Emphasising each 'no'.*) No! No! No! Don't always change the subject to start attacking me. I'm not accusing you of anything. I'm not asking you to wear calico or red flannel. All I'm asking is that when your son's in the room, you have the decency not to undress in front of him.

CLARISSE: (*Irritatingly calm.*) You're going too far. That's exactly what I went out of my way to avoid.

VENTROUX: (*Dumbfounded by her impudence, he looks at her, takes his head in his hands, as if to prevent it exploding, then goes upstage, waving his hands above his head.*) This is too much. You say I go too far?

CLARISSE: (*Going upstage towards him.*) Yes, I do. It's one more example of how unjust you always are. (*Coming downstage centre.*) Try to be nice to people. (*Sitting in the armchair near the fireplace with her back to the audience.*) I know how narrow minded you are, so, as you were both in my bedroom, I deliberately went and undressed in the bathroom.

VENTROUX: (*Seated on the sofa.*) Yes, but as soon as you
were in your underclothes, you came back into the
bedroom. I'd have preferred the reverse.

CLARISSE: I had to get my nightdress.

VENTROUX: Yes, yes. You've always a good reason for
everything. Why on earth do you have to wear your
nightdress at four o'clock in the afternoon?

CLARISSE: You are marvellous! It's obvious you didn't
have to go and die of heat at the Duchomier wedding.
(*Rising.*) And while we're about it, why did I go? Eh? For
your sake, not mine. (*Still talking, she reaches mid-stage.*) To
save you the trouble... as usual. I'm not a friend of the
girl's father. I'm not a deputy. You are. A fine way to
thank me!

VENTROUX: (*Shrugging his shoulders.*) It's not a question of
thanks...

CLARISSE: (*Cutting him short.*) I know, any thanks are due
to you. You've never thanked me. (*Going upstage
towards him.*) But that doesn't prevent me coming home,
soaked in sweat and wanting to make myself comfort-
able. I think I'm allowed to?

VENTROUX: Well, yes... I grant you that.

CLARISSE: (*Going upstage above the sofa.*) Thank you very
much. Oh, it's so cool here! You'd never believe that
outside we've at least ninety or a hundred degrees of...
latitude.

VENTROUX: (*Ironically.*) Latitude?

CLARISSE: (*Not understanding his meaning.*) A hundred
degrees, exactly.

VENTROUX: Of latitude? What do you mean, latitude?

CLARISSE: (*Above the sofa, slightly scornful.*) You don't
know what latitude is? (*Coming downstage.*) Well...
that's sad, at your age. (*Having reached the right of the
table, turning round and crushing him with her superiority.*)
Latitude means the thermometer.

VENTROUX: (*Mockingly.*) Oh? I'm sorry, I didn't know.

CLARISSE: I can't think why you went to a University.
(*Sitting on the chair, right of the table.*) When I think that

with a hundred degrees... of latitude, you still keep
us in Paris! Simply because you're a deputy and you
can't leave the Chamber before the end of the session!
Really! As if the Chamber couldn't get along
without you!

VENTROUX: (*Leaping to his feet.*) I don't know whether
the Chamber could get along without me or not. What
I do know is that when one accepts a job one does it.
A fine thing it would be if every deputy went off on
holiday because the Chamber didn't actually need him
personally. You'd have to close the place down. (*He goes
upstage.*)

CLARISSE: Splendid! Things wouldn't be any worse.
Whenever the Chamber's on holiday, the country's
always completely quiet. So...

VENTROUX: (*Having come downstage left of the table,
emphasising his words.*) My dear Clarisse, we are not in
the Chamber so that the country can be quiet. That is
not why we're elected. Anyway, it's got nothing to do
with it! I ask you why you're walking about in a
nightdress and you start criticising Parliament.
There's no connection between the two. (*He sits down
facing her.*)

CLARISSE: I'm sorry, there is. It's because of this
Parliament of yours that we're still in Paris with a
hundred degrees... of latitude.

VENTROUX: (*Ironically.*) You're sure?

CLARISSE: Of course I am. Because of these hundred
degrees... of latitude, I'm covered in sweat. Because
I'm covered in sweat, I had to change my underclothes. And because I changed my underclothes, you
get furious.

VENTROUX: I'm not furious because you changed your
underclothes. I'm furious because you were walking
about in front of our son in underclothes that were
transparent.

CLARISSE: (*Almost shouting.*) Is it my fault if they're
transparent?

VENTROUX: No. But it is your fault if you walk into your bedroom wearing them.

CLARISSE: This is the limit. I'm not allowed into my own bedroom now?

VENTROUX: I never said that. Don't make me say what I didn't say.

CLARISSE: (*Not listening.*) where to do you want me to take off my clothes? In the kitchen? The pantry? In front of the servants? Oh! Then you'd start screaming like a polecat.

VENTROUX: You're twisting the argument...

CLARISSE: (*Rising and going upstage towards the sofa.*) No, I'm not. I was in my own room. You had no right to be there. I didn't ask you in, did I? (*Sitting on the sofa.*) If my clothes upset you, you simply had to leave.

VENTROUX: (*Rising.*) Ha! There's logic for you!

CLARISSE: It's the truth. Making a scene because I came into my bedroom in my underclothes! (*Almost shouting.*) What did you want me to do, my night-dress was there!

VENTROUX: (*Going to her.*) I was there. You only had to ask me. I'd have fetched it.

CLARISSE: (*With disconcerting logic.*) Then it was the same thing. You'd have seen me with nothing on.

VENTROUX: I'm your husband.

CLARISSE: He's my son.

VENTROUX: (*Seizing his hair as if about to tear it out.*) It's hopeless. (*To CLARISSE.*) So you think that's the same?

CLARISSE: Well... practically.

VENTROUX: Oh!

CLARISSE: After all, what about you? You're a stranger... to me. You're my husband, but that's a convention. When I married you... I can't think why...

VENTROUX: (*Bowing.*) Thank you.

CLARISSE: ...I didn't know you. Then, bang, suddenly, because we said yes in front of a fat old man with a tricolour scarf round his waist, it's allowed. You saw me with nothing on. That's indecent.

VENTROUX: You think so?

CLARISSE: But my son! He's my flesh. My blood. Well... if the flesh of my flesh sees my flesh, that's not indecent. (*Rising.*) Unless you're prejudiced.

VENTROUX: Is that all? Prejudiced?

CLARISSE: (*Passing in front of him: haughtily.*) And small minded. Thank heaven I'm above that.

VENTROUX: (*Collapsing into the armchair next to the fireplace.*) She's above that! It's the same with everything.

CLARISSE: (*Returning to the charge as she goes to the sofa and sits.*) No, but I mean... since he was a tiny baby, he's seen me get dressed twenty-five thousand times, hasn't he? And you've never said anything.

VENTROUX: All the same, the day arrives when these things have to stop.

CLARISSE: (*Exasperatingly calm.*) Yes. I agree.

VENTROUX: Well, then!

CLARISSE: (*Looking at the ceiling.*) Good... when?

VENTROUX: When what?

CLARISSE: (*As before.*) What day? What hour?

VENTROUX: What do you mean, what day, what hour?

CLARISSE: Do they stop? There must be one day, one particular hour. Why today specially? Why not yesterday? Why not tomorrow? So I'm asking what day? What hour?

VENTROUX: (*Repeating in the same tone.*) What day? What hour? The questions she asks! How do I know? I can't say exactly.

CLARISSE: You can't say exactly! (*Rising and advancing on him.*) You can't say exactly! That's marvellous! But you expect me, a woman, who by definition is less intelligent than you, or so you say, you expect me to be able to, when you admit you can't.

VENTROUX: (*Beyond himself.*) You're talking nonsense.

CLARISSE: (*Reaching the left.*) No, I'm not. You're attacking me, I'm defending myself.

VENTROUX: (*Rising and going towards her.*) What are trying to prove? That it's all right for a mother to appear in front of her son in her underclothes?

CLARISSE: (*Leaning back against the front of the table, left.*)
I'm not complaining about that. You don't like it. All
right, you only have to tell me without getting angry.
I'd do what you want.

VENTROUX: (*Scarcely convinced.*) You'd do what I want!
(*Sitting right of the table.*) You know you wouldn't! You
can't not wander about in your underclothes. You
can't help it.

CLARISSE: You're exaggerating.

VENTROUX: Every day.

CLARISSE: I don't. You may see me like that sometimes
in the morning, because I haven't got dressed, but
once I am dressed, I assure you...

VENTROUX: That you're *not* just in your underclothes.
Obviously. But you never are dressed.

CLARISSE: (*Getting angry.*) You mean you don't want me
to get dressed?

VENTROUX: Yes, yes. Get dressed, but stay in the
bedroom to do it. And close the door. You always
leave it open. It's not decent for the servants.

CLARISSE: They don't come in.

VENTROUX: They've no need to, they only have to look.

CLARISSE: Servants! It doesn't mean anything to them.

VENTROUX: Doesn't it? They're men like anyone else...
You are extraordinary. You leave the door open when
you're dressing. And close it to put your veil on.

CLARISSE: (*With cramped little niggling gestures.*) Yes,
because I don't like being disturbed when I'm putting
my veil on. I can't stand people moving around, I can
never finish.

VENTROUX: (*Rising and going upstage above the sofa.*) It's a
pity you don't feel the same about washing. That's
even worse. You turn on the bathroom light and don't
draw the curtains.

CLARISSE: (*Indignantly.*) When?

VENTROUX: Yesterday.

CLARISSE: (*Suddenly calm.*) Oh yes, I did.

VENTROUX: You're like an ostrich. Because you can't
see out, you imagine other people can't see ·in.

CLARISSE: (*Going to the table and leaning back against it, unconcerned.*) Who do you think looks?

VENTROUX: Who? (*Pointing to the window.*) Clémenceau. Clémenceau lives across the way and spends all his time at the window.

CLARISSE: Pah! Clémenceau's seen lots of women.

VENTROUX: Possibly. Possibly. He may have seen lots of women, but I'd rather he didn't see you. I would be in trouble. (*He sits on the sofa.*)

CLARISSE: How?

VENTROUX: How? You don't know Clémenceau. He's our leading comedian. With the wit of a street urchin. He's terrible. If he makes a joke about me or gives me a nickname, he'd ruin me.

CLARISSE: You've nothing to worry about. He's in your party.

VENTROUX: That's the point. Your enemies are always in your own party. If he were on the Right, I wouldn't give a damn... nor would he. But on the same side we're rivals. Clémenceau thinks he might become a minister again. And I might too.

CLARISSE: (*Surveying him.*) You?

VENTROUX: (*Rising.*) You know that. You know in one of the recent regroupings, after my speech on agriculture, I was offered... the Ministry... for the Navy.

CLARISSE: (*Sitting right of the table.*) Oh, yes...

VENTROUX: Minister for the Navy! I must say! Can you see me?

CLARISSE: Not remotely.

VENTROUX: (*Vexed.*) Naturally.

CLARISSE: Minister for the Navy! You can't even swim.

VENTROUX: What difference does that make? You don't have to be able to swim to handle affairs of state.

CLARISSE: Poor affairs of state!

VENTROUX: (*As he speaks, moving upstage left so that he can come downstage left of the table.*) I can't think why I discuss it with you. No man's a prophet in his own country. Luckily people who know me think differently. (*Sitting on the chair left of the table and facing her.*) But please! Don't

wreck my career at this particular moment by thought-
less behaviour which could be disastrous.

CLARISSE: (*Shrugging her shoulder.*) Disastrous!

VENTROUX: Remember you're the wife of a future
minister. When I am a minister, will you go parading
round the corridors of the ministry in your nightdress?

CLARISSE: No, of course not.

VENTROUX: I say minister. But you never know. That's
the beauty of the Republic, Everyone can hope to
become President. If I become President! (*Raising his
hand as if to parry an objection.*) Imagine! We'd entertain
kings... queens. Would you receive them in your nightdress?

CLARISSE: No, no.

VENTROUX: Would you appear like this?

CLARISSE: Of course not. I'd put on my dressing gown.

VENTROUX: (*Rising and holding his head in his hands.*) Her
dressing gown! She'd put on her dressing gown!

CLARISSE: Well, I'd put on whatever you wanted.

VENTROUX: (*In front of the table.*) Poor girl, this is
frightening. You've no idea how to behave.

CLARISSE: (*Drawing herself up indignantly.*) I haven't?

VENTROUX: (*Indulgently, putting his hand on her shoulder in
a friendly manner.*) I'm not angry. With you it's not
deliberate, you're just ingenuous. But the results are
sometimes the same. (*He moves to the right.*)

CLARISSE: Oh! Give me one example. One example of
my behaving incorrectly.

VENTROUX: I don't have to look far. Yesterday when
Deschanel was here.

CLARISSE: Well?

VENTROUX: Not five minutes after I'd introduced him,
you could think of nothing better to say than 'Oh, what
funny material your trousers are made of! What is it?'
And you start feeling his bottom. (*He adds the gesture to
the words.*)

CLARISSE: (*Escaping.*) Bottom, bottom! It was the material!

VENTROUX: Yes, but his bottom was underneath. Do
you think that's a proper way to behave?

CLARISSE: What do you want me to do? I couldn't ask him to take his trousers off, I'd never seen him before.

VENTROUX: (*Opening his arms wide.*) All right, all right. But you didn't have to feel the material. Deschanel's surely done enough in politics for you to find something else to talk about besides his trousers. Especially with supporting gestures!

CLARISSE: (*Reaching the extreme left.*) Oh! You see wrong in everything!

VENTROUX: (*Shrugging his shoulders as he goes upstage.*) Yes, I see wrong in everything.

CLARISSE: (*Turning round sharply and going to sit at the left of the table, facing him.*) You're very critical about other people, I advise you to look to yourself. You talk about my behaviour, What about yours... the other day... at the picnic... with Mademoiselle Dieumamour?

VENTROUX: Mademoiselle Dieumamour?

CLARISSE: You sucked her neck! Do you think that's a proper way to behave?

VENTROUX: (*Seizing his forehead in both hands.*) Oh, no! No! When women start writing history...! (*He sits, right of the table.*)

CLARISSE: You didn't suck her neck?

VENTROUX: (*Vehemently.*) Yes, I sucked her neck. Of course I sucked her neck. I sucked her neck and I'm proud of it. It's entirely to my credit.

CLARISSE: You think so?

VENTROUX: You don't think I was overcome by desire, inspired by her forty summers and the smallpox marks on her nose...?

CLARISSE: You never know with men. They're so depraved.

VENTROUX: Yes, oh, of course... She'd been stung and the bite looked nasty. I couldn't let her be poisoned and die, out of respect for social conventions.

CLARISSE: (*Shrugging her shoulders.*) Poisoned! How did you know the bite was poisonous?

VENTROUX: (*Cuttingly.*) I didn't know. But it might have been, so I didn't hesitate. A sting can kill you, if it isn't cauterised or sucked immediately. There was nothing to

cauterise it with. So I sacrificed myself. I did what
Christian charity demanded. (*A wide gesture.*) I sucked
her neck.

CLARISSE: That's very convenient. With that system you
can go around sucking the neck of every woman you
like the look of, by pretending she's been stung by a
poisonous insect.

VENTROUX: What are you trying to make out? You
think I did it for pleasure?

CLARISSE: (*Not convinced.*) No. No.

VENTROUX: For the next two hours my mouth was full
of the taste of stale powder and candle wax. I ought to
be praised.

CLARISSE: Oh, yes. Yes. Everything other people do is
wrong. But with you it has to be admired. (*She rises.*)

VENTROUX: I didn't say that.

CLARISSE: (*Above the table, leaning towards her husband who
is still seated.*) If I'd sucked Monsieur Deschanel's neck...
Whew!... What a row you'd have made. (*She goes downstage to the right.*)

VENTROUX: Yes, naturally.

CLARISSE: There you are! What did I say? (*Planting
herself in front of him.*) Do you call that justice?

VENTROUX: (*Taking her hand and nodding his head as he
smiles indulgently.*) You know, your method of arguing is
quite disarming.

CLARISSE: It's true!

VENTROUX: (*Pulling her towards him, emphasising his
words.*) Yes, yes, you're right. You're always right. I'll
never suck her neck again.

CLARISSE: (*Quickly.*) I'm not asking that. If she's ever
stung again, poor woman, it's your duty...

VENTROUX: There. You see you agree with me.

CLARISSE: (*Very close to him, whimpering.*) You know, you
upset me too. You say such wounding things. Then
I can't help it, I get angry.

VENTROUX: I say wounding things?

CLARISSE: Yes. That I walk about with nothing on. And
suck Monsieur Deschanel's neck.

VENTROUX: I never said that.

CLARISSE: No, pinched his bottom.

VENTROUX: But dammit, when you do something I don't approve of, I'm entitled to tell you.

CLARISSE: (*Leaning against his knee.*) Perhaps you are, but you could do it nicely. You know, when you speak to me gently, you can make me do anything you like.

VENTROUX: All right then. Nicely. For my sake, please don't always walk about undressed.

CLARISSE: Very well then, yes. Say it like that.

VENTROUX: Splendid. That's how I like to hear you talk.

CLARISSE: (*Her head on his shoulder.*) You see how sensible I am, when you're nice.

(*VICTOR enters, walking straight into the room from the hall.*)

VICTOR: (*Seeing CLARISSE in her nightdress on VENTROUX's knees and turning quickly away.*) Oh!

CLARISSE: (*Turning round and seeing VICTOR.*) Oh! (*She rushes towards the window, almost knocking over VICTOR, who, with his back turned, is in her way.*)

VENTROUX: (*Still seated, but drawing himself up on the palms of his hands.*) Eh? What? Who's there?

VICTOR: (*Without turning round.*) Me, sir.

CLARISSE: (*At the window, pulling the bottom of the curtain round her without undoing the loop.*) Don't look. Don't look.

VICTOR: (*Blasé, having seen lots of women.*) Oh...

VENTROUX: (*Furiously as he crosses the stage.*) Ohhh! 'Don't look! Don't look!' About time!

CLARISSE: (*To calm him.*) I'm behind the curtain.

VENTROUX: (*In front of the sofa.*) What does that matter? He's seen you in your nightdress now.

VICTOR: (*On the left. Blasé as before.*) Oh... I've been here for months...

VENTROUX: (*Coming downstage, right.*) I see. It's not the first time he's seen you in your nightdress. Charming!

CLARISSE: (*On the extreme right.*) I assure you.

VENTROUX: (*Going upstage near the sofa.*) Oh, leave me in peace. When you know I don't like something...

VICTOR: (*Reassuring.*) Don't worry, sir, I've my own girl, so...

VENTROUX: (*In between them, rushing towards him.*) What did you say? You've your own girl! Do you think my wife...?

VICTOR: (*Protesting.*) Oh, sir...

VENTROUX: Anyway, what is it? What did you want?

VICTOR: To tell you a gentleman called this morning and left his card.

VENTROUX: (*Snatching the card.*) Who was that? (*He passes, grumbling, to the left.*) Sticking his nose in everywhere... (*Reading the card.*) No! It can't be true! Good God! He was here? Him?

VICTOR: Him, exactly.

VENTROUX: (*Calling him to order, rudely.*) What him? Who do you mean, him?

VICTOR: (*Unperturbed.*) Him. Well, this gentleman. He said he'd call again at 4.30.

VENTROUX: (*Nodding, with a smile that lights up his whole face.*) Well, I must say... (*Turning round, he sees VICTOR next to him, also nodding and smiling approvingly.*) Will you get the hell out of here!

VICTOR: (*Moving away.*) Yes, sir.
   (*VICTOR goes out.*)

CLARISSE: (*Emerging from behind he curtain and sighing with relief.*) Ah!... Phew!

VENTROUX: (*Coming downstage to the armchair, right.*) You may well say Phew. I'm not sorry about this.

CLARISSE: (*Having passed along the length of the sofa in order to come downstage centre.*) Oh, good! I was afraid you'd be annoyed.

VENTROUX: (*Appalled by this interpretation.*) What!... (*Furiously.*) I am annoyed. Of course I'm annoyed.

CLARISSE: (*Going towards him.*) Then why did you say you're not sorry?

VENTROUX: (*As before.*) I'm not sorry because it may teach you a lesson. (*He sits angrily in the armchair near the fireplace.*)

CLARISSE: (*In front of the fireplace.*) Oh! I didn't understand. I thought you were saying something nice.

VENTROUX: To encourage you?

CLARISSE: Never mind, it was only a trifle (*Leaning towards him.*) Who's the man who left his card?

VENTROUX: (*Grumbling.*) Only a trifle! Is that all you think it was?

CLARISSE: Do you expect me to start tearing my hair out? Who is this man...?

VENTROUX: (*Raging.*) What? Who? What man?

CLARISSE: The man who left his card.

VENTROUX: (*Angrily, as he rises.*) What's that got to do with you? (*He reaches midstage.*)

CLARISSE: (*Hurt.*) I beg your pardon. (*She sits in the place he has just vacated.*)

VENTROUX: (*Coming back towards her.*) All right, if you must know, it's a man I'm thankful didn't see you talking to your servant in your nightdress. My reputation in my constituency would have been ruined. (*As he speaks, he sits on the sofa.*)

CLARISSE: Why?

VENTROUX: If I gave him a chance to gossip... (*Changing his tone.*) He's the man who led the most bitter campaign against me at the last election.

CLARISSE: No! Not Monsieur Phartillon?

VENTROUX: The mayor of Moussagnac, in person!

CLARISSE: No! The man who led the campaign for your opponent, the Marquis de Berneville?

VENTROUX: The unified socialist. Exactly.

CLARISSE: (*Rising and reaching the left.*) Well! What impertinence! (*Leaning back against the front of the table.*) The man who kept calling you a damp imp!

VENTROUX: (*Looks at her, astonished, then slowly rises and goes towards her. When he reaches her, he says ironically.*) What did you say?

CLARISSE: (*Completely naturally.*) Damp imp.

VENTROUX: (*Laughing.*) Damp imp! (*Correcting her.*) Damned pimp!

CLARISSE: (*As before.*) He didn't say damp imp?

VENTROUX: (*Tit for tat.*) He didn't say damp imp.

CLARISSE: I always heard damp imp.

VENTROUX: You always heard wrong.

CLARISSE: So that's why I didn't understand.

VENTROUX: (*Ironically.*) That's why, obviously.

CLARISSE: Anyway I don't care. Damp imp or damned pimp, I hope you'll kick him out with all the honours he deserves.

VENTROUX: On the contrary I shall be as charming as possible. And if you see him, I'd be glad if you (*With emphasis.*) would be too.

CLARISSE: (*Surprised.*) Oh!

VENTROUX: Phartillon in my house! This is my revenge! He may be a filthy bastard...

CLARISSE: Oh! Yes, bastard.

VENTROUX: But we must remember he's a very big businessman. He employs five or six hundred people in his factory, he can influence their votes. We must be nice to him. You have to be practical in life. (*Taking out his watch.*) It's nearly four thirty, he won't be long. go and get dressed. (*He makes her move across to the right.*)

CLARISSE: (*Going upstage.*) Yes, of course. (*Changing her mind and coming downstage above the sofa.*) Oh! (*She goes to the bell and rings it.*)

VENTROUX: (*Having reached the left.*) What are you doing?

CLARISSE: Ringing for Victor.

VENTROUX: (*Ironically.*) Don't you think he's seen enough of you?

CLARISSE: (*Gently beating the air with her hand, as if slapping him.*) Naughty!... I want him to take the tray away. (*She goes round the sofa to the front of the small table with the coffee on it.*) I keep on telling him to take away the cups when we've finished coffee. It's awful seeing them lying about. Besides they attract flies. And wasps. There. Look at that. (*She picks up the front of her nightdress and waves it in front of the table.*) Shoo! Shoo! Flies, wasps, the lot of you! (*To VENTROUX.*) I can't bear untidiness. I like everything to be correct.

VENTROUX: (*Pointing at her.*) She likes everything to be correct!

CLARISSE: (*Having gone upstage above the sofa.*) Now, as
I don't want Victor to see me in my nightdress...

VENTROUX: (*Mocking.*) No, really?

CLARISSE: (*With the same slapping gesture as before.*) Don't
tease me. (*Ringing the bell.*) When he comes, you'll tell
him to take it all away, won't you?

VENTROUX: I shouldn't bother. The bell doesn't work.
There's something wrong with the battery.

CLARISSE: It's probably dried out. The poor thing's
thirsty. You only have to fill it up with water.

VENTROUX: Possibly. I know nothing about them. (*He
goes upstage.*)

CLARISSE: I'll give it a drink.

VENTROUX: Good. Hurry up.

CLARISSE: Yes.

(*CLARISSE goes out upstage right. As VENTROUX closes
the door, he opens it again.*)

VENTROUX: (*Calling.*) And put on your dressing gown!

CLARISSE: (*Off.*) Yes. You know, when you ask me nicely,
I'm delighted... (*Her voice is lost in the distance.*)

(*VENTROUX closes the door and stands there for a
moment. He raises his eyes to heaven and makes a significant
gesture with his head and hand. He holds his forehead in his
hand for a moment, then goes to the window and suddenly
notices something.*)

VENTROUX: Oh! (*Waving his hand.*) Hullo, hullo! (*To the
audience with a bitter laugh.*) Clémenceau! (*Furiously he
draws the lace curtain.*) Has that man nothing to do!
(*The bell rings offstage.*)

Ah! Now for him! (*He has by now crossed the stage and
going upstage left of the table, takes up a dignified position
against it.*)

(*VICTOR enters.*)

VICTOR: (*Right of VENTROUX.*) Monsieur Phartillon.
(*PHARTILLON enters and stops in the doorway, slightly
hesitant.*)

VENTROUX: (*Distantly, without turning his head.*) Come in.

PHARTILLON: (*Advancing.*) Excuse me...

VENTROUX: (*As before. To VICTOR.*) You may go.

(*VICTOR looks at him with amazement and goes out.*)
(*Coldly and comtemptuously.*) Please sit down.

PHARTILLON: (*Right of the table.*) My dear deputy...

VENTROUX: (*Stopping him with a gesture.*) 'Dear'...?

PHARTILLON: (*Having started to sit down, standing up again.*) Why ever not?

VENTROUX: (*Stiffly.*) After your campaign against me!

PHARTILLON: Oh... Campaign...

VENTROUX: For three months you said I was a criminal, a police spy, totally corrupt and completely decadent.

PHARTILLON: (*Quickly spreading out his hands as if to grip those of VENTROUX.*) That doesn't in any way detract from my very great respect for you.

VENTROUX: (*Caustically.*) Highly honoured! (*Seeing PHARTILLON is about to sit down, he begins to do the same, but immediately stands up when he sees PHARTILLON has stopped.*)

PHARTILLON: What do you expect? I must admit you weren't my candidate. (*He begins to sit down.*)

VENTROUX: I noticed that. (*He begins to sit down, but stands up when he sees PHARTILLON is not sitting.*)

PHARTILLON: My man was the Marquis de Berneville.

VENTROUX: (*With a forced laugh.*) You're entitled to your choice.

PHARTILLON: You understand. He's an old friend of mine. A unified socialist like me. And he held my daughter at her christening...

VENTROUX: Really.

PHARTILLON: There were lots of reasons.
(*He starts to sit down, but immediately stands up.*)
(*VENTROUX does the same.*)
Quite apart from the fact that he's a multi-millionaire and in the interests of my people... You understand, don't you?

VENTROUX: Please don't defend yourself.

PHARTILLON: Anyway you won.

VENTROUX: For me that's what matters.

PHARTILLON: Of course.

(*As before they both start to sit down and stand up again.*) Anyway that's all over and done with. Now we're not candidate and voter. I am the Mayor of Moussagnac, come to pay a friendly call on his Deputy to ask him to intervene with the appropriate ministry. I never for a moment doubted you'd welcome me warmly.

VENTROUX: You were right. (*Facing him, back to the audience.*) In fact I was just saying to my wife...

PHARTILLON: Do forgive me. I haven't asked you how she is. Won't I have the honour of meeting her?

VENTROUX: (*Moving away and passing to the centre.*) I'm afraid you're unlucky. My wife's getting dressed. And with women, you know... That takes a long time.

PHARTILLON: (*Reaching the left.*) What a pity!

CLARISSE: (*Off.*) You think you've taken away the cups!... You think you've taken away the cups!

VENTROUX: (*Going upstage at the sound of her voice and immediately speaking louder.*) No, listen, I've slandered her. I can hear her voice. (*Coming downstage.*) Dressed already! It's a miracle.

PHARTILLON: I'll be delighted...

(*CLARISSE, dressed as before, bursts in from the hall followed by VICTOR. She goes straight to the small table.*)

CLARISSE: All right. Come and see how you've taken away the cups.

VENTROUX: (*Turning round.*) Darling, I... (*Seeing her clothes.*) Ohhh!

CLARISSE: (*Jumping at his shout and, instinctively turning round to escape, bumping against the sofa and falling onto it on her knees.*) Oh!... You frightened me.

VENTROUX: (*Rushing towards her and whispering.*) For God's sake! Will you get out of here! Get out of here!

CLARISSE: (*Astonished, as she stands up.*) What's the matter?

VENTROUX: Have you gone mad? Coming in here in a nightdress when I've got visitors?

CLARISSE: (*To PHARTILLON over VENTROUX's shoulder.*) I am sorry. I didn't hear the bell.

PHARTILLON: (*Gallant.*) I'm not complaining.

VENTROUX: (*Drawing back a little to give free play to his gestures of indignation.*) Aren't you ashamed of yourself? Appearing like that with a servant at your heels?

CLARISSE: (*Half whispering in the most natural way.*) It's because Victor hadn't taken away the cups.
(*To VICTOR.*) There, look how you've taken them away.

VENTROUX: (*Losing his temper.*) I don't give a damn about the cups. (*To VICTOR.*) Get the hell out of here. (*He pushes him out.*)

VICTOR: Yes, sir.
(*VICTOR goes out.*)

CLARISSE: (*Coming downstage to PHARTILLON while VENTROUX is getting rid of VICTOR.*) I don't know if you're like me, but when I see cups...

VENTROUX: (*Jumping at her and making her move to the right.*) Yes, yes, fine, run along. Quickly. Get out.

CLARISSE: (*Having been virtually swept into his arms as he pushes her towards the door, releasing herself.*) Really! Don't talk to me like that. I'm not a dog.

VENTROUX: (*Going upstage and tearing out his hair; back to the audience.*) Ohhh!

CLARISSE: Well, I'm not. (*Suddenly changing her manner as she comes downstage towards PHARTILLON, while VENTROUX closes the door upstage; very graciously.*) Monsieur Phartillon, I presume?

PHARTILLON: (*Left of table.*) Yes I am, yes.

VENTROUX: (*Turning round, dumbfounded.*) What!

CLARISSE: (*Very much mistress of the house.*) Delighted to meet you. Won't you sit down?
(*As she speaks she sits right of the table, while PHARTILLON sits on the left, facing her.*)

VENTROUX: (*Running to her.*) No, no, no! You're not going to receive him dressed like that?

CLARISSE: (*Unperturbed, as she rises.*) Oh! Of course. It is a little unusual!

VENTROUX: (*To the audience, shrugging his shoulders.*) Unusual!

CLARISSE: But really it was so hot. (*Putting both hands flat on the back of PHARTILLON's hands which are on the table.*) Look, feel my hands. See how hot they are.

VENTROUX: (*Opening his arms wide.*) All right. All right. Don't start behaving like you did with Deschanel.

CLARISSE: (*Her hands still on PHARTILLON's, stretching forward across the table.*) What do you mean? It's his hand, not his bottom.

PHARTILLON: What?

CLARISSE: I want to show him how hot mine is.

PHARTILLON: (*Misunderstanding; appalled.*) Your bott...?

CLARISSE: (*Immediately understanding his confusion and correcting him quickly.*) My hand! My hand!

VENTROUX: (*Seizing her by the arm and pushing her to the right.*) Yes all right! He doesn't care a damn about your hand.

PHARTILLON: (*Quickly, very gallant.*) I do, I do.

CLARISSE: (*Rubbing her arm which has been bruised by her husband's brutality.*) There. You see.

VENTROUX: (*Erupting and marching on her, driving her upstage.*) Yes, all right, that's enough. Do please go away.

CLARISSE: (*Going upstage.*) All right. All right. But then there was no point in asking me to be charming.

VENTROUX: (*Coming back downstage.*) Who asked you to be charming?

CLARISSE: You did. You did. You said 'If you see Monsieur Phartillon...'

VENTROUX: (*Scenting the gaffe, leaping towards her and whispering quickly.*) Yes, splendid. Splendid.

CLARISSE: (*Merciless.*) What to you mean 'splendid'? (*Continuing.*) '...please be as charming as possible...'

VENTROUX: (*Going towards PHARTILLON, protesting.*) No, I didn't. I didn't.

CLARISSE: (*As before.*) This is too much. You actually added: 'He may be a filthy bastard'...

VENTROUX: (*Moving as if he'd been kicked.*) Oh!

PHARTILLON: (*Nodding and smiling maliciously.*) Oh?

CLARISSE: (*Continuing pitilessly.*) '...but he's a big businessman with five or six hundred employees. We must be nice to him!'

VENTROUX: (*Speaking at the same time, to drown her voice.*)

No, no, I didn't. I never said that. Monsieur Phartillon,
   I hope you don't believe her.
PHARTILLON: (*Indulgently.*) Pah! Of course you said it.
VENTROUX: I didn't. I didn't.
CLARISSE: (*Over her husband's shoulder.*) Monsieur
   Phartillon! I hope you'll do me the honour of believing
   me.
VENTROUX: (*At the limit of exasperation, spinning round on
   her.*) You're getting on my nerves! (*Pointing to the door.*)
   Get to hell out of here. Go on, get out.
CLARISSE: (*Going upstage.*) Really! Please don't talk like
   that.
VENTROUX: (*Not permitting another answer.*) Go on, clear
   out.
CLARISSE: (*Obeying, but still trying to prove she's right.*) Yes,
   but don't you dare say you didn't...
VENTROUX: (*As before.*) Get on out!
CLARISSE: I won't get on out, if you don't know what
   you said.
VENTROUX: (*Pushing her out.*) I said get out!
CLARISSE: (*Terrified, escaping.*) Ohhh!
   CLARISSE goes out. VENTROUX slams the door.
VENTROUX: (*Coming downstage, furious.*) Ohhh!
   (*As he arrives downstage, the door opens. CLARISSE enters
   and comes downstage immediately behind him.*)
CLARISSE: Monsieur Phartillon, I didn't say goodbye.
   Delighted to have met you.
PHARTILLON: (*Bowing.*) The pleasure is mine.
VENTROUX: (*Whirling round at the sound of her voice and
   dashing at her, as if about to kick her.*) For God's sake!
CLARISSE: (*Scurrying away, frightened.*) I was only saying
   goodbye...
   (*CLARISSE goes out. VENTROUX slams the door behind
   her. He stands for a moment, stunned, and takes his head in his
   hands as if to stop it exploding. Then he comes downstage
   towards PHARTILLON, who is standing in front of the table.*)
VENTROUX: I'm appalled. Appalled.
PHARTILLON: (*Offhand.*) Oh...

VENTROUX: (*On the right.*) Please don't believe a word she said. It was a joke. 'Bastard'. You don't believe I said that!

PHARTILLON: Never mind. I said you were a criminal, totally corrupt, completely decadent.

VENTROUX: Yes, I know. I'd have been entitled to. But even so... You see, my wife... do please excuse her. Really the way she appeared...

PHARTILLON: (*Extremely polite.*) Entirely to her advantage.

VENTROUX: You're too polite. Please do believe she doesn't usually wander about, dressed like that. But today, it's so hot, isn't it? It is almost forgivable. You felt her hands, you could see...

PHARTILLON: Yes, yes.

VENTROUX: I must say, I... Feel mine. (*Manipulating PHARTILLON's hand between both of his.*) They're covered in sweat.

PHARTILLON: (*Disengaging his hand and wiping it against his coat.*) Yes... yes.

VENTROUX: It's most unpleasant.

PHARTILLON: (*Finishing wiping his hand, with feeling.*) Most unpleasant!

VENTROUX: So naturally my wife... She was so hot, she... she felt the need to change into... into... how shall I put it?... Well, there's no other word... a nightdress.

PHARTILLON: I quite understand.

VENTROUX: I'm sure you do. (*Going upstage.*) I'm sure you do.

PHARTILLON: If only I could do the same!

VENTROUX: (*Turning round; without thinking.*) Please do. Please do.

PHARTILLON: Eh? No... No... Really I...

VENTROUX: (*Coming downstage.*) No. No. Of course.. So, you see... She didn't hear the bell, so naturally... she came in.

PHARTILLON: Please.

VENTROUX: She thought she was alone.

PHARTILLON: (*As though it was the most natural thing in the world.*) Yes... With the servant.

VENTROUX: (*Repeating after him without thinking.*) With the ser... (*Disconcerted.*) Ah yes, the... the servant... (*Trying to appear offhand.*) Well, the servant, yes, naturally, there is... there is a reason.

PHARTILLON: Naturally.

VENTROUX: If her were an ordinary servant, of course...

PHARTILLON: Of course, if he were an ordinary servant...

VENTROUX: But the fact is... they were brought up together.

PHARTILLON: You don't say!

VENTROUX: (*With assurance.*) He's... he's her foster brother. Her foster brother.

PHARTILLON: (*Approving.*) Her foster brother.

VENTROUX: So, you see, a foster brother...

PHARTILLON: (*Going upstage, left of the table.*) Doesn't count, of course.

VENTROUX: That's what I say. He doesn't count... He doesn't... (*In a hurry to change the conversation.*) Anyway what can I do for you? This is just gossiping. What have you come to see me about? (*As he talks, he sits, right of the table.*)

PHARTILLON: (*Sitting opposite him.*) The Paris express. It stops at Morinville and goes straight through Moussagnac... which is quite as big.

VENTROUX: Indeed it is.

PHARTILLON: So we've decided to try to make the express stop at our station.

VENTROUX: (*Shaking his head.*) Ah! That's difficult.

PHARTILLON: (*Unperturbed.*) Don't say that. Twice we've had the chance to see it could be done.

VENTROUX: The express has stopped there?

PHARTILLON: Twice... Once it was derailed. And once it was sabotaged.

VENTROUX: Oh?

PHARTILLON: And the service wasn't affected at all.

VENTROUX: I see... That is an argument.

PHARTILLON: But unfortunately it doesn't happen regularly. So our people can't rely on it.

VENTROUX: Yes... You'd like a scheduled stop. Right.
I'll see what I can do. Send me a short statement.
In the meantime, so I won't forget, I'll make a note...
(*As he speaks, he picks up the memo pad; writing.*) Monsieur
Phart-ill-on.

PHARTILLON: (*Having risen, looking at what he has written.*)
Good. Good. (*Suddenly, quickly.*) No! No!... Not an F!
(*Spelling.*) P-H-A-R-T!

VENTROUX: (*Embarrassed.*) Oh! I am sorry. P-H. P-H.
Please believe me, it was quite unintentional.

PHARTILLON: (*Good natured.*) Don't worry. I'm used to it.
It's the spelling everyone thinks of first.

VENTROUX: (*Facetiously.*) Very *natural.*

PHARTILLON: (*Laughing.*) Yes. Yes.
(*Voices and banging can be heard beyond the hall door,
including indistinctly the following lines:*)

CLARISSE: (*Off.*) That's right. Give me the hot water bottle.

VICTOR: (*Off.*) Here it is.

CLARISSE: (*Off.*) Ah! Keep hold of me. Don't let go. Be
careful.

VICTOR: (*Off.*) I've got you. I've got you.

VENTROUX: (*Having listened for a moment, speaking above
their conversation.*) What on earth's going on? Can't we
have a moment's peace? (*He goes quickly to the door and
opens both halves – the actor playing VICTOR having released
the bolt holding the right half.*) What is it now?
(*CLARISSE can be seen perched on the top of a pair of steps,
her upper half hidden above the doorway. VICTOR is stretched
out, with his legs on the ground astride the steps, holding
CLARISSE firmly with both hands on her bottom.*)
(*With a shout, as he starts back, moving to the right of the
door.*) Ohhh!

CLARISSE: (*Bending down at her husband's shout, so that her
head appears, and holding a hot water bottle; very naturally.*)
Oh! It's you!

VENTROUX: (*On the extreme right, his voice choking with
indignation.*) What are you doing there?

CLARISSE: (*As before.*) Can't you see? I'm mending the
battery.

VENTROUX: (*Foaming at the mouth.*) What the hell are you two up to? Why are you holding my wife like that?

VICTOR: So she won't fall.

VENTROUX: What!

CLARISSE: Yes... If nobody holds me, I get giddy.

VENTROUX: (*Rushing at VICTOR.*) For God's sake! Can't you see you've got both hands on her bott... on her... It's indecent!

VICTOR: (*Unconcerned.*) Oh...

VENTROUX: (*Shaking him.*) Will you let go of her! Let go! (*He pulls him away.*)

CLARISSE: (*Nearly losing her balance.*) Oh! Do be careful. You'll make me fall.

VENTROUX: (*Brutally making her come down.*) Then come down. What are you doing up there? What's it got to do with you? (*He forces her downstage to the extreme right.*)

CLARISSE: (*Having handed the hot water bottle to VICTOR, when she reached the bottom of the steps.*) He doesn't know how to.

VENTROUX: Let him learn. Dressed like this! (*Coming downstage to PHARTILLON, who is in front of the table, and appealing to him.*) Is it decent, eh? Is it decent?... With the servant.

PHARTILLON: Well... as it's her foster brother.

VENTROUX: (*With a start.*) Oh!

CLARISSE: Who?

VICTOR: Me?

VENTROUX: (*Red with rage, leaping at VICTOR.*) Yes, you! What do you mean, 'Me'?
(*He pushes VICTOR towards the door, sending him up against the steps so that he almost falls down.*)
Go away. Who asked you to interfere in other people's business?

VICTOR: Yes sir.
(*VICTOR goes out – and must immediately refix the bolt on the outside.*)

VENTROUX: (*Slamming the door after him.*) I'll end up sacking the fellow. (*Coming downstage to PHARTILLON.*)

I must explain, he is her foster brother... he is her foster brother, but... not by the same father.

PHARTILLON: Not by the same father?

VENTROUX: (*Taken aback.*) Eh? (*Recovering.*) No, no. Let me explain. When I say 'Not by the same father', I mean... I mean... (*Exasperated at not finding an explanation, exploding.*) I'm fed up with you and your questions. What's it got to do with you?

PHARTILLON: But... But...

VENTROUX: Obviously I only tolerate this because I've good reason to.

PHARTILLON: I must point out I haven't asked any questions.

VENTROUX: Yes. But I know how it is. You don't ask any questions, but once you're back home with that Marquis of yours, you'll natter, natter, natter.

PHARTILLON: No, I won't. I wouldn't dream of it.
(*VENTROUX has walked across to CLARISSE.*)

CLARISSE: (*Very calmly to VENTROUX.*) You really ought to take a grip on yourself.

VENTROUX: (*Out of control.*) For God's sake. Will you go and get dressed.

CLARISSE: Yes, all right. Just give me a moment.

VENTROUX: (*Going upstage.*) Give you a moment! Give you a moment! For the last hour I've...

CLARISSE: Yes, but now Monsieur Phartillon's seen me. (*She goes upstage above the sofa on the right, to talk to PHARTILLON, who has also moved upstage during the preceding lines.*)
Well, Monsieur Phartillon! I'm in my nightdress, I know. But am I indecent? Do I show any more than in a ball dress?

PHARTILLON: (*Conciliating.*) No, indeed.

VENTROUX: (*Between them, sitting in despair on the chair to the left of the hall door.*) Ha! You think so, do you?

PHARTILLON: Actually, in your nightdress with your hat on, you almost look as though you've been paying calls.

CLARISSE: There! Do you hear? It's true. (*Turning round so that she can be seen from every side.*) What can you see, I ask you? What can you see?

PHARTILLON: Oh, nothing. Though actually I can see your silhouette underneath, because you're in front of the window.

VENTROUX: (*Leaping at her and dragging her away from the window.*) Ohhh!

CLARISSE: (*As she is pulled away.*) Ah! Because of the window! (*To VENTROUX.*) You are rough. (*To PHARTILLON.*) But apart from that?

PHARTILLON: Oh! Apart from that, nothing.

CLARISSE: (*Sitting on the sofa.*) There. I'm delighted. (*Screaming and leaping to her feet.*) Ohhh!

PHARTILLON: What?

VENTROUX: What is it now?

CLARISSE: (*Distressed.*) I don't know. I felt as though I'd been stabbed.

VENTROUX: Stabbed?

CLARISSE: It went straight to my heart. (*She turns round and a wasp can be seen on her left buttock.*)

VENTROUX: Your heart? Is that where your heart is? (*He pulls off the wasp and shows it to her, holding the wings.*) This is what stabbed you. You've been stung by a wasp. (*He puts it on the floor and crushes it with his foot.*)

CLARISSE: (*Choking and screaming.*) A wasp! Ohhh! I've been stung by a wasp!

PHARTILLON: I am sorry.

VENTROUX: (*Furious, but delighted.*) Splendid! That will teach you to walk about with nothing on! (*He comes downstage extreme left.*)

CLARISSE: (*Going to the small table.*) Look. It's your fault. I told you, if you leave cups lying about...

VENTROUX: (*As before.*) A good thing too! It may teach you a lesson.

CLARISSE: (*Indignantly.*) Good thing! He's glad! Glad! (*Panic-stricken.*) Ohhh! A wasp! Perhaps it's poisonous! (*VENTROUX goes and sits on the chair at the right of the table, while PHARTILLON, to avoid getting embroiled in the conversation, has gone upstage and pretends to be examining the pictures.*)

VENTROUX: No, no.

CLARISSE: (*Going to him.*) Julien! Julien, please? (*Turning round to present her bottom to him and starting to lift up her nightdress.*) Suck it, won't you? Suck it.

VENTROUX: What? (*Pushing her away.*) Have you no thought for me?

CLARISSE: Julien! Julien! Be kind! (*Returning to the charge.*) Suck it, please! Suck it.

VENTROUX: (*Pushing her away again, as he rises to come downstage left.*) Oh, shut up.

CLARISSE: Please, do suck it. You did for Mademoiselle Dieumamour.

VENTROUX: (*Coming back towards her.*) In the first place it was her neck, not her... And it was a fly. Not a wasp. (*He goes upstage.*)

CLARISSE: (*Choked with emotion.*) But a wasp's as dangerous. Didn't you see in the paper two days ago a man died of a wasp sting.

VENTROUX: That was different. He swallowed one. It choked him.

CLARISSE: (*By the armchair next to the fireplace.*) I might choke. Oh! I'm choking. I'm choking.

VENTROUX: (*Not worrying, sitting on the sofa.*) No, you're not. It's just fancy.

CLARISSE: I am, I am. (*Collapsing into the armchair and immediately letting out a cry of pain.*) Ohhh! (*Going to her husband.*) Please, Julien... (*Turning round as before to present him with her bottom.*) Suck it, do. Suck it.

VENTROUX: (*Between her and PHARTILLON, pushing her away.*) No, no. You're getting on my nerves.

CLARISSE: (*Distraught.*) Oh, you're heartless. What can I do? (*Seeing PHARTILLON, who is coming downstage, still engrossed in his examination of the ornaments.*) Ah! (*Coming downstage towards him.*) Monsieur Phartillon!

PHARTILLON: (*Turning round towards her.*) Yes?

CLARISSE: (*Turning round to present her bottom.*) Please, Monsieur Phartillon. Please.

PHARTILLON: Me?

VENTROUX: (*Leaping at her and dragging her away.*) Are you out of your mind? You're asking him now?

CLARISSE: Why not? I'd rather do that than die.

PHARTILLON: Of course I'm very honoured, but really I...

CLARISSE: (*Returning to him.*) Monsieur Phartillon, in the name of Christian charity!

VENTROUX: (*Seizing her by the arm and forcing her to turn round.*) Stop it.

CLARISSE: (*Thus presenting Phartillon with the relevant part of her anatomy.*) Please?... Please?

PHARTILLON: Really, I assure you! Don't ask me.

VENTROUX: (*Exploding and dragging her midstage.*) Shut up. Go and do it yourself. (*He releases her and goes to the right.*)

CLARISSE: (*Tears in her voice.*) How can I?

VENTROUX: (*Returning towards her.*) Well... put a poultice on it. Anything. But stop bothering us.

CLARISSE: (*Clenching her hands in front of her face.*) Go away. Go away. I can't bear the sight of you. If I die, it will be your fault.

VENTROUX: (*Sitting in the armchair, right.*) All right, it will be my fault.

CLARISSE: There's men for you! (*She rushes out, upstage left, calling.*) Victor! Victor!
(*CLARISSE goes out, slamming the door behind her.*)

VENTROUX: (*Collapsed in the armchair.*) She ought to be locked up. Locked up.

PHARTILLON: (*Standing in front of the table, left; after a moment's hesitation.*) Monsieur Ventroux!

VENTROUX: What?

PHARTILLON: You do forgive me, don't you? I didn't think it was my duty to...

VENTROUX: (*Not believing his ears.*) What!

PHARTILLON: Really, we hardly know each other...

VENTROUX: Of course.

PHARTILLON: Exactly. That's what I thought.

VENTROUX: This is the last straw!

CLARISSE: (*Off.*) All right. Wait till I tell my husband. Wait till I tell my husband.

VENTROUX: Oh, no! What's she up to now?
(*CLARISSE bursts in, followed by VICTOR.*)

CLARISSE: (*Back to the audience; to VICTOR.*) You're cowards all of you. (*Turning towards her husband and PHARTILLON.*) And murderers. Victor's no better than you two.

VENTROUX: Eh? What is it now?

CLARISSE: (*Behind the sofa.*) He wouldn't suck it either.

VENTROUX: Victor!

VICTOR: (*In the doorway, sheepishly.*) Sir, I didn't dare to.

VENTROUX: For God's sake! Are you asking everyone to suck your bottom?

CLARISSE: Oh! It's throbbing. Throbbing. My whole cheek must be swollen.

VENTROUX: Go to the dentist.

CLARISSE: Not my face!

VENTROUX: Then go to the doctor.

CLARISSE: Yes. There's a doctor on the floor above.

VENTROUX: (*Sitting in the armchair he has just got out of; angrily.*) He's not a doctor, he's a public health officer.

CLARISSE: It's the same sort of thing. Victor! Victor, go upstairs and get him.

VICTOR: Very good.

CLARISSE: (*Her hand on the sting.*) Ohhh! I'll go and put a poultice on it.

(*CLARISSE goes out into her own room, still clutching herself.*)

VICTOR: (*In the doorway, after a moment's hesitation, when he sees CLARISSE has gone.*) You're not angry, sir, because I didn't...

VENTROUX: Not you too! (*Pushing him out.*) Will you... will you go and get that man upstairs.

VICTOR: (*Rushing towards the front door, leaving the drawing room door open.*) Yes, sir, yes.

(*As VICTOR is about to open the front door, the bell rings. VICTOR opens the door and bumps into DE JAIVAL, who is waiting in the doorway.*)

DE JAIVAL: Oh! You're very quick at answering the bell.

VICTOR: Sir?

DE JAIVAL: Monsieur Ventroux, please.

VENTROUX: (*From the drawing room.*) Come in. What is it you want?

DE JAIVAL: Ah! Forgive me. (*Coming downstage.*) I am
  Monsieur Romain de Jaival of the Figaro.
VENTROUX: Ah! Of course. (*To VICTOR, who is in the
  doorway.*) All right. Go away.
VICTOR: Yes, sir.
  (*VICTOR goes out, closing the door behind him.*)
VENTROUX: (*On the right.*) What can I do for you?
DE JAIVAL: (*Centre.*) My paper's sent me to ask you for an
  interview.
VENTROUX: Aha!
DE JAIVAL: About politics in general... Since your recent
  speeches you're very much in the public eye.
VENTROUX: (*Flattered.*) Thank you...
DE JAIVAL: I'm only saying what everyone's thinking...
  Especially your new draft bill, 'Working Class
  Confinements'. Free childbirth and the midwife state!
VENTROUX: Yes. Most interesting. It's a cause I have
  very much at heart.
DE JAIVAL: I want to do something exciting, picturesque,
  out of the ordinary. I write special features. You may
  have read them...
VENTROUX: Of course I have, of course. Monsieur de...
DE JAIVAL: Jaival. Romain de Jaival.
VENTROUX: De Jaival, of course. I'm completely at your
  service. I must just finish off a small matter with this
  gentleman. (*Introducing.*) Monsieur Phartillon!
DE JAIVAL: (*Bowing.*) Phartillon?
PHARTILLON: (*Quickly.*) With a P-H.
VENTROUX: The mayor of Moussagnac.
DE JAIVAL: I know, of course.
PHARTILLON: (*Surprised and flattered.*) Me?
DE JAIVAL: I passed through it once.
PHARTILLON: Oh! Moussagnac... Yes, yes. No, I thought
  you... Yes, yes.
VENTROUX: So, if you'd care to wait a moment, I'll take
  this gentleman into my study and be with you in five
  minutes.
DE JAIVAL: Please, please. If you don't mind, I'll sit down
  and make a few notes while I'm waiting.

VENTROUX: (*Very gracious.*) Make yourself at home.

DE JAIVAL: (*Coming downstage to go round the table and sitting on the chair at its left.*) Thank you.

VENTROUX: This way, my dear Mayor.

PHARTILLON: After you, my dear Deputy.

> (*VENTROUX and PHARTILLON go out. DE JAIVAL, at the table, has taken out his notebook. He casts an eye round the room to memorise it and starts taking notes.*)

CLARISSE: (*Off.*) He's not here yet?

> (*CLARISSE enters from her room and comes downstage without seeing DE JAIVAL.*)
>
> What on earth's the man doing?

DE JAIVAL: (*Unable to suppress his surprise at seeing a woman in a nightdress.*) Oh!

CLARISSE: (*Turning round.*) Ah! Here he is. (*Going to him.*) Quickly, doctor, quickly.

DE JAIVAL: (*Surprised by the title.*) What?

CLARISSE: (*Taking his hand and dragging him towards the window.*) Quick, come and look at it.

DE JAIVAL: (*Letting himself be led across the room.*) Look at what?

CLARISSE: My sting.

DE JAIVAL: Your sting?

CLARISSE: (*Pulling the curtain cord.*) Let's draw back the curtain so you can see better.

DE JAIVAL: (*Not understanding what she is leading up to.*) Oh?... Yes, yes.

CLARISSE: You'll see, doctor...

DE JAIVAL: (*Stopping her.*) I'm sorry, I'm not a doctor.

CLARISSE: (*Behind the sofa.*) Yes, yes, I know all about that. I don't mind. Look at it. (*She pulls up her nightdress.*)

DE JAIVAL: (*Having been facing the audience, turning round at the invitation and then jumping in amazement.*) Oh!

CLARISSE: (*Her body bent forward, her nightdress tucked up and her right arm on the back of the sofa.*) You see?

DE JAIVAL: (*Laughing, surprised.*) Oh, yes.. Yes, I do see. I do see.

CLARISSE: Well?

DE JAIVAL: (*To the audience, delighted.*) Picturesque! Exciting! What an opening paragraph!

CLARISSE: (*Turning her head to one side, without changing her position.*) What?

DE JAIVAL: Do you mind if I take a few notes?

CLARISSE: No, no, no... Go on, feel it.

DE JAIVAL: You want me to...?

CLARISSE: Feel it. So you'll know.

DE JAIVAL: (*More and more surprised.*) Oh?... Yes, yes. (*He is facing the audience and, reversing his left hand, he feels her right side. Aside.*) Very exciting!

CLARISSE: Not there. The other side.

DE JAIVAL: (*Moving his hand to the other side.*) Oh, I'm sorry.

CLARISSE: I've been stung by a wasp.

DE JAIVAL: There? Oh!... What impudence!

CLARISSE: The sting must still be in it.

DE JAIVAL: No!

CLARISSE: Go on, look at it.

DE JAIVAL: (*Getting used to the situation.*) Oh! You want me to... Yes. Yes. (*He screws his monocle in his eye and squats down.*)

CLARISSE: Can you see it?

DE JAIVAL: Wait. Yes, yes. I can.

CLARISSE: Oh? Oh?

DE JAIVAL: Yes, yes, It's sticking so far out, I think with my nails I...

CLARISSE: Try, doctor, try.

DE JAIVAL: Yes, yes.

(*PHARTILLON enters from the study, followed by VENTROUX.*)

PHARTILLON: (*Seeing what's happening.*) Oh!

VENTROUX: (*Scandalized.*) Ohhh! (*He rushes to PHARTILLON and makes him turn round.*)

CLARISSE: (*Unperturbed, not changing her position.*) All right. All right.

DE JAIVAL: (*Pulling out the sting and rising.*) Look. Here it is. Here it is, the brute.

VENTROUX: (*Leaping at DE JAIVAL and sending him whirling away to centre.*) For God's sake!

CLARISSE & DE JAIVAL: (*Together.*) What is it?

VENTROUX: Showing your bottom to a reporter from the
  Figaro!

CLARISSE: The Figaro? The Figaro?

VENTROUX: (*Furious.*) Yes. Monsieur Romain de Jaival
  from the Figaro.

CLARISSE: (*Advancing on DE JAIVAL as though she's furious
  with him.*) De Jaival! You're Monsieur De Jaival?
  (*Changing her tone; very slowly.*) What an amusing article
  you wrote in the paper yesterday! (*To her husband.*)
  Didn't he?

VENTROUX: (*Raising his arms to heaven.*) Look. Look.
  That's how much it matters to her! (*His eyes wander to
  the window and he sees the lace curtains drawn back; shouting.*)
  Ohhh!... Clémenceau!

CLARISSE: Clémenceau!

VENTROUX: (*Coming downstage as if drunk.*) Clémenceau!

CLARISSE: (*Looking where he's pointing.*) Oh, I see! (*She
  smiles and nods a greeting to the invisible Clémenceau!*)

VENTROUX: He's laughing! Roaring with laughter!
  (*Falling onto the sofa.*) I'm finished! My political career's
  ruined!
  (*As the curtain falls, CLARISSE makes little bows to
  CLEMENCEAU.*)

CLARISSE: Good afternoon, Monsieur Clémenceau.
  I'm very well Monsieur Clémenceau. How are you,
  Monsieur Clémenceau? Ah! I'm so glad. So glad,
  Monsieur Clémenceau.

CURTAIN